School **Money** Matters
A Handbook for Principals

Davida W. Mutter
Pam J. Parker

Association for Supervision and Curriculum Development
Alexandria, Virginia USA

Association for Supervision and Curriculum Development
1703 N. Beauregard St. • Alexandria, VA 22311-1714 USA
Telephone: 800-933-2723 or 703-578-9600 • Fax: 703-575-5400
Web site: http://www.ascd.org * E-mail: member@ascd.org

Gene R. Carter, *Executive Director;* Nancy Modrak, *Director of Publishing;* Julie Houtz, *Director of Book Editing &
Production;* Katie Martin, *Project Manager;* Shelley Young, *Senior Graphic Designer;* BMWW, *Typesetter;*
Tracey A. Smith, *Production Manager.*

All Web links in this book are correct as of the publication date below but may have become inactive or otherwise
modified since that time. If you notice a deactivated or changed link, please e-mail books@ascd.org with the words
"Link Update" in the subject line. In your message, please specify the Web link, the book title, and the page number
on which the link appears.

Printed in the United States of America.

s1/04

ISBN: 0-87120-813-X • ASCD product # 103057 • List Price: $34.95
($27.95, ASCD member price, direct from ASCD only)

Library of Congress Cataloging-in-Publication Data

Mutter, Davida W., 1946–
    School money matters : a handbook for principals / Davida W. Mutter,
Pam J. Parker.
        p.   cm.
Includes bibliographical references and index.
        ISBN 0-87120-813-X (alk. paper)
    1. Education—Finance—United States—Handbooks, manuals, etc.   2.
School principals—United States—Handbooks, manuals, etc.   3.
Bookkeeping—Handbooks, manuals, etc.   I. Parker, Pam J., 1952–   II. Title

    LB2825.M83 2004
    371.2'06—dc22   2003023468

13 12 11 10 09 08 07 06 05 04   12 11 10 9 8 7 6 5 4 3 2 1

School **Money** Matters:
A Handbook for Principals

Contents

ACKNOWLEDGMENTS

I owe a special debt of gratitude to Pam, my highly competent co-author and the most courageous person I know, and to my loving husband, David, for sharing his day-to-day knowledge of the principalship.

—D. W. M.

So many people have influenced my life and made this book possible. There is my co-author, Davida, a skilled educator and knowledgeable school finance professional. And then there is my loving and wonderful family—my husband, Johnny, who is my best friend and has always encouraged me; my daughter and son-in-law, Angela and Patrick, who have given me two wonderful grandsons, Ric and Noah; and my parents and parents-in-law, who have always been there for us.

—P. J. P.

A special thanks from both of us to Joseph Daniels for the use of his company's allCLEAR software in creating the graphic organizers for the draft version of this book; to Anne Meek, our ASCD development editor, for her encouragement and great suggestions; and, most especially, to W. Randolph Nichols, superintendent of Chesapeake Public Schools, for his leadership and integrity in the handling of public school funds.

Preface

Today's school leaders are typically selected for their accomplishments and potential for improving student achievement. It is an appropriate priority; after all, the purpose of school is to promote learning. At the same time, school administration requires the "wearing of many hats." In addition to attending to instructional matters, principals and assistant principals every day oversee the operation of their facilities, maintain safe environments, communicate with parents, implement discipline procedures, address staff concerns and development needs, and supervise student activities. In the midst of all this, they are also responsible for managing their school's finances.

School money management is a particularly complex process, because it is a subset of a district's overall budget allocation and reflects major state and district educational policies pertaining to how individual schools may spend funds. What's more, today's school money management usually involves computerized accounting programs, which may intimidate school leaders who lack practical understanding of accounting concepts, and thus contribute to those leaders' willingness to pass the responsibility on to their bookkeeping staff.

As tempting as it can be to entrust financial matters almost entirely to bookkeepers, it is just not a wise practice. School money really matters, and unless administrators pay attention to the ongoing, daily responsibilities of school bank accounts, vending services, school stores, fund-raising events, and the like, they risk failure in a major responsibility. Financial mismanagement (including loss of funds or embezzlement by a staff member) is not only damaging to an administrator's career, it can seriously undermine community relations and public confidence in the school. What's more, the time-consuming task of rectifying costly financial problems presents a further diversion from educational leadership.

Although financial management *is* important, school leaders cannot permit themselves to be consumed by it; it is not the goal of schooling, but a means of "getting things done." What is needed, then, is a clear, practical source of immediate information, based on sound accounting principles and operational integrity that can put exemplary school financial management within the reach of administrators and teachers alike. We knew of no publication that fills this need, so we decided to write one ourselves.

In *School Money Matters,* we address fiscal management issues at the school level: those financial matters affecting school activity funds (i.e., club, instructional, flow-through, and major school accounts) that are the responsibility of the principal, with the help of other staff. This book applies directly to the stewardship responsibility in Standard 3 of the Standards for School Leaders recently adopted by the Interstate School Leaders Consortium: "The administrator has knowledge and understanding of principles and issues relating to fiscal operations of school management" (Council of Chief State School Officers, 1996, p. 3).

Conversely, this book does not take up central office administrators' responsibility for the development and implementation of districtwide operational and capital budgets, nor does it speak to the federal, state, and local regulations that typically apply to these funds. These topics, addressed in public school finance courses, are of interest to all aspiring school administrators, but they do not usually explain the accounting principles that most concern busy administrators: the financial matters that affect the school's day-to-day operations.

To enhance the book's usefulness as a desk resource for new, aspiring, and practicing principals, we have organized it in short, single-topic-focused chapters. Graphic organizers and samples of filled-in financial forms clarify complex accounting concepts; electronic versions of these forms (created in Microsoft Excel, downloadable, and ready for use) are included on the accompanying CD-ROM. We offer three appendixes: a year-round checklist of the principal's key financial activities, a collection of sample financial forms, and a guide to using this book's electronic forms. Finally, we include a glossary of useful financial management terms, collecting the definitions provided within the various chapters in a single location for easy reference. Our hope is to help you, the reader—a new, aspiring, or practicing principal—to fulfill your stewardship responsibility for public funds at the school level, so that you have more time to focus your attention on what really matters most: student learning.

1

Activity Fund Safeguards

Activity Fund Safeguards—*General accounting procedures designed to meet three important school financial objectives: (1) to protect school staff from suspicion of theft or laxness, (2) to protect school assets, and (3) to fulfill the stewardship responsibility for public funds expected by the general public.*

Activity fund safeguards are the general "internal control" procedures all schools need to protect their assets from loss, misuse, or theft. These procedures assist with the prevention or timely detection of unauthorized transactions and help assess a school's compliance with required policies, regulations and laws, such as Internal Revenue Service (IRS) rules and state purchasing laws (U.S. General Accounting Office, 1999).

Overall, internal control procedures apply to accounting and record-keeping practices at the school. They provide reasonable assurance that financial records are reliable and that "assets are safeguarded from unauthorized use" (Virginia Department of Education, 1989, p. 4). Internal control procedures apply to all aspects of your school's financial operation and address such functions as the receiving of funds from students and parents, the disbursement of funds to pay bills, and the securing of financial documents such as receipt books and checks. In general, these safeguards are recognized best business practices to protect both school assets and staff. Setting and adhering to internal controls helps you to fulfill your stewardship responsibility for public funds. See Figure 1.1 for a graphic summary of these points.

Guidelines for Spending School Activity Funds

Before discussing activity fund safeguards, it is best to understand the guidelines for spending activity funds (Virginia Department of

FIGURE **1.1**

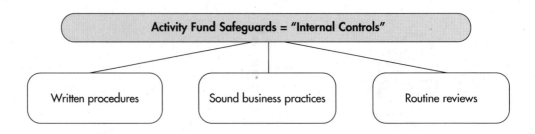

Education, 1989). Always follow these rules, unless your district and state have issued explicit, written exceptions. The most important thing to remember is that the use of school activity funds is *restricted*. These funds are not yours to lend, borrow, or spend in any way that you see fit.

- Use school activity funds only for the purpose for which those funds have been raised or allocated.
- Use school activity funds raised by the entire student body to benefit the student body as a whole.
- Encourage student representation, with faculty supervision, in the management of funds raised by a student group.
- Spend activity funds on the students who were in school at the time the funds were raised.
- Prohibit fund-raising projects that conflict or detract from the instructional program or that pose a risk to student safety.
- Manage school activity funds in accordance with sound budgetary and accounting procedures.

Characteristics of a Sound Internal Control System

Sound internal control systems require the right balance between control and practicality. Here are several general principles of a sound internal control system to assist you in the assessment of your current system of safeguards (Business Against Crime, 2001).

Reasonableness

The cost of a control should not exceed the control's benefit. Remember to consider cost in terms of money, time, restrictions on staff (e.g., overly complex purchasing procedures), and public opinion.

- *Money.* An example of a control that increases costs is employing two bookkeepers at every school to allow for separation of duties (i.e., receipt of funds and payment of funds). Depending on the amount of cash receipts per year, this control may or may not be reasonable. For example, in a secondary school with cash receipts in excess of $750,000 per year, it may be cost effective (and therefore, reasonable) for the district to spend a fraction of that amount to hire a second bookkeeper.

– *Time.* Requiring staff to issue individual receipts for all funds received (e.g., issuance of individual receipts for small library fines) is an expensive use of time that may not add substantive internal control, and is, therefore, excessively restrictive.

– *Public opinion.* Marking special events such as field day or the first day of class by giving school employees gifts (e.g., t-shirts) paid for with school funds may increase faculty morale at the cost of public opinion regarding the handling of school funds. (See Chapter 10: Gifts to Students or Staff.) On the other hand, never allowing special occasion gifts of token value is excessively restrictive.

Timeliness

To be effective, a control must be applied at the right time. For example, failure to balance the bank statement every month defeats the purpose of the control, which is to detect and correct errors immediately.

Reality

Does the procedure really provide a safeguard? Locking a supply closet, but allowing all staff free access to the key does not accomplish the desired control.

Commitment

Protecting school assets requires consistency from both the school's administrative leadership and the district's administrative leadership. Within the school, an effective internal control is foremost a "top-down" system that begins with you, the principal, and extends to all other members of the staff. Use effective judgment in applying controls and seek advice from district accounting or internal audit officials when you are in doubt about the viability of a procedure.

The Three Types of Internal Controls

There are three basic types of internal controls, and all are essential within a school accounting system to protect school assets and staff (Sawyer, Dittenhofer, & Scheiner, 1996). (See Figure 1.2 for a graphic summary.)

– *Preventive controls* are measures designed to discourage errors or irregularities *before* they occur. An example of a preventive control is the principal's approval of purchase orders prior to buying materials or equipment. Preventive controls are cost effective.

– *Detective controls* are measures designed to identify an error *after* it has occurred. The principal's monthly review of the school's bank statement to identify irregularities is a detective control. The after-the-fact nature of these controls makes them less cost-effective than preventive controls.

– *Corrective controls* are measures to ensure that problems located through detective controls are corrected. One example of a corrective control is when the principal finds a banking error and follows up in a timely manner to ensure that the error is explained and corrected.

FIGURE **1.2**

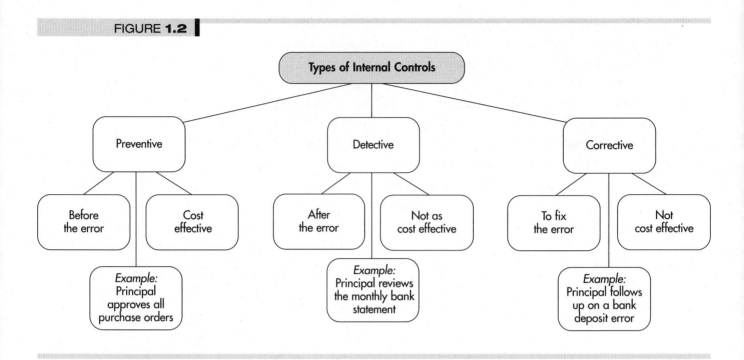

Basic General Controls for a School Accounting System

There are some basic, general safeguards that you, as the principal, can put in place to help protect school assets from loss and theft. They are common sense practices ranging from setting the financial management "tone" in your building to limiting staff access to your financial system.

➤ Create the Environment

As the principal, your attitude and actions define the business environment of the school (Institute of Internal Auditors, 2001). Your insistence on the following guidelines will communicate their importance in school operations and set the tone for the way in which all staff members view and handle financial matters. (See Figure 1.3 for a graphic summary.)

- Maintain high standards of integrity and ethical values; do not compromise standards, procedures, or policies with regard to money matters.

- Commit to the accounting procedures expected of all staff. Consistent application is critical because few bookkeeping and teaching staff have received formal training in accounting.

- Insist on highly competent bookkeeping staff and administrative staff.

- Avoid overreliance on the bookkeeper. Take warning if the bookkeeper is in total control or has the staff's "complete confidence." Restrict bookkeepers to working only when an administrator is in the building. A system based on trust is not a system.

- Make sure staff are aware of their responsibilities regarding school funds. A leading internal audit authority (Sawyer, Dittenhofer, & Scheiner, 1996) emphasizes that failure to place and maintain reasonable controls becomes the ally of dishonest employees and tempts honest ones to become dishonest.

FIGURE **1.3**

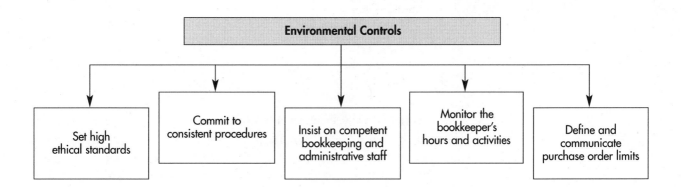

➤ Administrative Controls

Internal safeguards are of little value in your school if there is no effort on your part to ensure they are followed diligently. Follow the guidelines in this section faithfully (Parker, 2001). (See Figure 1.4 for a graphic summary.)

- Always review monthly bank statements and financial reports when they arrive.

- Ensure that accounts are reconciled in a timely manner (e.g., require financial reports to be prepared and submitted within a week of a fund-raising activity's conclusion).

- Keep unused control forms for bookkeeping (e.g., teacher receipt books, unused checks) locked in a secure location under the control of an administrator.

- When possible, separate financial duties so that no one person is responsible for the entire process (e.g., writing checks, signing checks, and preparing the bank reconciliation). If you have a very small office staff, try using other controls:

  - Increase administrative review procedures (e.g., the principal opens all bank statements and then forwards them to the staff member responsible for the bank reconciliation).
  - Increase the frequency of unannounced internal audits or accounting reviews (e.g., request that the district internal audit staff schedule an informal review of the bank reconciliation process).

Establish an "in box" for financial documents so that they do not get lost among other incoming mail.

FIGURE **1.4**

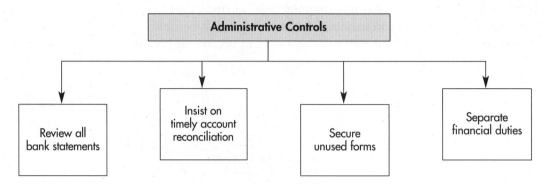

tip

Change your financial management system password at least every 90 days.

➤ **Limit Access to the Financial System**

• Restrict computer access to financial records by changing passwords frequently. Always use passwords that are combinations of letters and numbers. Don't use your pet's name or your favorite hobby as passwords, and never keep a written password in your desk, taped to your computer, or in other obvious locations.

• Backup all essential electronic data files and store the backups in a safe place away from school.

• Secure petty cash funds in an area with limited access. (See Chapter 13: The Petty Cash Fund.)

• Restrict staff access to the keys and combinations for office safes, lock boxes, deposit bags, and filing cabinets. Change safe combinations and locks when a member of the office staff leaves the school's employment. Bolt small office safes to the floor or wall (Washoe County [Nev.] Government, 1996).

Controls for Cash Receipts

Cash receipts—the money coming in to a school—are the assets most vulnerable to misuse or theft. The controls in this section are designed to provide assurance that funds are received, recorded correctly, and deposited promptly (Parker, 2002).

➤ **Preparing Deposits**

• The bookkeeper should post all receipts in the bookkeeping system without delay. Daily deposits are recommended, unless your total daily receipts are less than $25, in which case make deposits no later than Friday afternoon. Never keep money in the school building over the weekend.

• Separate the duty of receiving funds from that of depositing funds (e.g., teachers receive the funds and issue receipts; the bookkeeper deposits the funds). Separating these functions provides an excellent safeguard against unauthorized use of funds.

• Stamp checks received with "For Deposit Only" and the school's name and bank account number.

• Lock up money and checks received until the funds are deposited.

➤ **Making Deposits**

• Deposit total cash receipts when collected (Watts, Burkel, & Watts, 2001). Do not allow partial deposits, because a portion of the daily receipts could be used to cover temporary or long-term theft.

  – Daily deposits reduce the possibility that employees will "borrow" funds (e.g., staff IOUs).
  – Funds not deposited are not generating interest income as part of the school's total account balance.
  – Banks protect school funds from loss due to carelessness as well as misuse.

• Provide security measures to individuals taking deposits to the bank (e.g., vary deposit times; request security officers to accompany staff for evening deposits).

• Set up a monitoring system for bank deposits. Bank statements should not be available to the person making deposits because this person might remove funds and manipulate the bank reconciliation to cover the loss. Either designate someone other than the bookkeeper to make deposits or stipulate that you, as the principal, must sign each deposit slip before it goes to the bank. Always make a mental note of the size of the deposit.

• Review deposits posted to the bank statement to ensure that they accurately reflect projects, such as picture sales, where deposits are typically large.

• Require your bookkeeper to keep copies of filled-out bank deposit slips. The bank's records of deposits should agree with the school's deposit records.

• Cross-train staff members to make bank deposits.

➤ **Giving Receipts**

• Encourage parents, students, and staff members to obtain a receipt from school staff for transactions exceeding $3. Receipts leave a clear money trail.

• Instruct staff to issue prenumbered receipts for money received and to always use receipts in sequential order. Issuing receipts in random order destroys the audit trail.

• Prepare triplicate-style receipts and adhere to a standardized system of usage:

  – The original goes to the parent or student.
  – The second copy goes to the bookkeeper, along with the money.
  – The third copy remains with the teacher's receipt book.

• If it is necessary to void a receipt, all three copies of the receipt should be marked as "void."

Controls for Cash Disbursements

Cash disbursements, the money "going out" of your school, are properly made through checks (the actual payment) and purchase orders (the "promissory" payment, which sets aside funds until payment is due). The controls in this section are designed to provide assurance that school funds are not used or allocated for unauthorized purposes and to help you maintain accurate knowledge of your school's "true" bank balance.

➤ Issuing Checks

The correct way for a school to issue money to pay bills and reimburse staff for approved school-related expenses is to write a check. Checks leave a clearly numbered audit trail of the amount, date, and purpose of each disbursement.

- *Always* issue payments by check (i.e., no cash payments unless through a controlled petty cash fund; see Chapter 13: The Petty Cash Fund).

- Prohibit checks made payable to "Cash," as these checks can easily be used for unauthorized purposes.

- Use prenumbered checks, and issue them in sequential order.

- Require two signatures on all checks issued. The purpose of multiple signatures is to confirm decisions about whom to pay, when to issue payment, and how much that payment should be. For additional control, make the "second signer" someone other than the bookkeeper (e.g., an assistant principal).

- *Never* sign a blank check. Signed, blank checks are easily used for theft of school funds.

- When writing a check, use heavy, dark ink. Fill in any blank areas with a squiggly line, and do not use abbreviations. These measures will help prevent your checks from being chemically washed, which is a major means of organized theft (ABC News, 2002).

- Write "Void" on voided checks, and then tear off the signature lines. This extra precaution will prevent the checks from being cashed in the event that the "void" is chemically removed. Instruct your bookkeeper to save all voided checks for audit review.

- Mail signed checks to vendors, parents, and others from a post office or from a locked mailbox. Do not leave checks to be mailed on the office counter or in an "outbox" overnight.

- Restrict access to unused checks by locking them in a secure location under the control of an administrator.

- Never write school checks to cover personal expenses or cash personal checks. School money is for *school purposes only*.

➤ Issuing Purchase Orders

- Follow your district or state purchasing regulations with regard to when price quotes or formal bids are required. In some states (e.g., Virginia), public employees who violate these guidelines are subject to automatic dismissal (*Code of Virginia*, 2002).

- Use prenumbered purchase orders to record the encumbrance (i.e., the obligation of funds); see Chapter 7: Encumbrance of Funds.

- Always require a written, approved purchase order to authorize a purchase. This practice ensures that funds are available to cover the cost of the item or service.

– Use computerized purchase orders when possible. The preferred way to follow *open purchases* (i.e., purchase orders that have been issued to a vendor but have not yet been paid) is to use a software package that tracks each purchase order from the time of issuance until payment.

– In a computerized system, the purchase order software and the bookkeeping software are integrated into one package that automatically (1) generates the proper number of copies and sets aside funds for the entered account, (2) tracks purchase orders by number, and (3) tracks purchases by vendor.

- Whether using a manual system or computerized purchase order system, follow these guidelines:

– Each purchase order should be a multiple-copy document (Meigs & Meigs, 1992). The original goes to the vendor or supplier; one copy is sent to the department or teacher requesting items; one copy is maintained by the bookkeeper.

– Prohibit prepayments to vendors, or control them through written guidelines (i.e., limit the amount, the type of purchases allowed, and documentation required).

– Review open purchase orders monthly to ensure that items ordered are still needed. Cancel or inquire about any open purchase order that is more than three months old. Stale purchase orders tie up school funds needlessly.

➤ Determining the School's True Balance

- Begin by requiring the preparation of the bank reconciliation as soon as the bank statement arrives.

- Review the bank reconciliation statement each month without fail.

- Compare the bank balance to the school's financial statement for the same month. The bookkeeper should provide written documentation to explain any differences between the bank balance and the school's financial statement.

- Know your true fund balances. School *activity fund* accounts are typically classified into three subcategories: (1) *school accounts* (e.g., instructional accounts, general fund, school store); (2) *student accounts* (e.g., club accounts, team accounts); and (3) *flow-through accounts.*

– The total of the balances in the *school accounts,* after obligated funds (encumbrances) have been subtracted, is the only general money available to operate the school. The only way to be sure that you have sufficient funds is to routinely perform this review process!

– The money in *student accounts* must be spent on the projects for which the funds were raised (e.g., field trips). This money is not available for general school projects or specific items, such as cell phones or copiers.

– *Flow-through accounts* (e.g., summer school funds) may be received at your school, but they must be forwarded to the central office, not spent at the school level.

Summary

As an administrator, you will find it helpful to commit to basic internal control procedures for the consistent handling of school funds. With routine application, these safeguards increase your confidence as a money manager and take up less of your time. All staff will have clear direction with regard to your expectations for receiving and disbursing school funds. Remember that control procedures are of little value if there is no effort to determine whether or not safeguards are being used. A system that is based on trust alone is not sufficient to protect your school funds or to protect your school staff from suspicion concerning loss or theft.

2

Admission Tickets

Admission Tickets—
*Prenumbered tickets sold to
control entrance to a school
event. Profits from the ticket
sales are used for the benefit
of a particular student group
or the student body as a
whole. Ticket sales apply
to athletic games, school
dances, fairs, plays, or other
events where admission is
controlled.*

The sale of tickets to events is common in schools. In order to
determine profit (or loss), schools need to follow specific procedures to account for unsold tickets, sold tickets, and the money
collected. Many schools are casual in the handling of admission
tickets, and because tickets are paid for with cash, this is an area
vulnerable to theft. Additionally, schools that use cash from the
immediate sale of tickets to pay the people serving as ticket takers
may be in serious violation of Internal Revenue Service (IRS) rules
regarding the payment of payroll taxes. Following the procedures
in this chapter will help ensure proper accounting for funds and
compliance with federal regulations.

Financial Controls for Ticket Sales

In all cases in which money is collected for ticket sales at school
or at a school-sponsored event, financial safeguards or "controls"
are needed to ensure that funds are not lost, misused, or stolen.
Here are some guidelines to follow. (See Figure 2.1 for a graphic
summary.)

- Designate one person to be the event coordinator for each type
  of controlled-admission event (e.g., an athletic coordinator, a
  school dance sponsor). To maintain a system of checks and balances between receiving funds and preparing deposits, the
  bookkeeper should *not* serve as a event coordinator.

- Use prenumbered tickets to control admission and to assist in
  reconciling the money collected with the number of tickets
  sold. You may also opt to

Electronic ticket boxes can be a great investment. They operate like a cash register by recording the money collected and issuing the purchaser a prenumbered ticket or receipt.

– *Use two-part tickets.* The ticket buyer receives one part of the ticket, and the ticket seller retains the other part to reconcile the money collected with the tickets sold.

– *Use computerized tickets.* An electronic device prints a ticket stub for the buyer and records the sale in electronic memory.

- Require individual ticket sales reports (see p. 14) in order to reconcile the number of tickets sold to the amount of money collected.

- Store the unsold ticket inventory in a locked area with limited key access.

- Prepare a financial report (see p. 15) at the end of the event to summarize the event's receipts and expenses and to determine the profit or loss.

FIGURE **2.1**

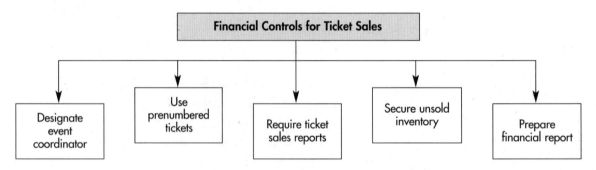

- **Financial Controls for Ticket Sales**
  - Designate event coordinator
  - Use prenumbered tickets
  - Require ticket sales reports
  - Secure unsold inventory
  - Prepare financial report

Responsibilities of the Event Coordinator

The event coordinator is responsible for safeguarding funds collected and unsold tickets. As principal, make sure that the event coordinator performs the following tasks promptly after an event where tickets have been sold. (See Figure 2.2 for a graphic summary.)

- Review the individual ticket sales reports completed by each ticket seller.

- Secure the ticket inventory throughout the event to prevent unsold tickets from becoming damaged or lost (i.e., the storage area should be locked with limited access). To reconcile tickets sold with the money collected, it will be necessary to know the numbers of the first and last tickets sold.

- Secure the funds collected at the end of the day, or, if tickets are sold at the event itself, at the end of the event (e.g., forward the money to the bookkeeper for deposit; make a night deposit, if necessary). Adhere to district guidelines regarding the amount of money a school can keep in the building overnight.

- Reconcile ticket sales with the money collected by comparing the total tickets sold on each ticket sales report to the money received.

- Prepare the event's financial report and submit it for administrative review.

FIGURE **2.2**

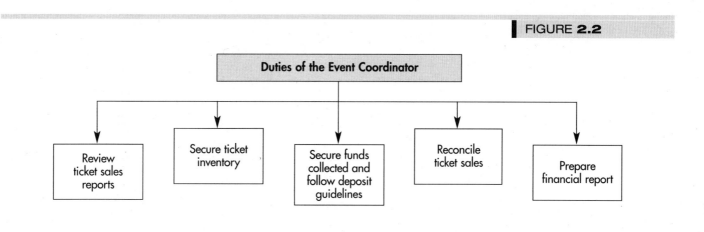

Duties of the Event Coordinator

- Review ticket sales reports
- Secure ticket inventory
- Secure funds collected and follow deposit guidelines
- Reconcile ticket sales
- Prepare financial report

Using a Change Fund

When selling admission tickets, a change fund is usually necessary to provide ticket buyers with the appropriate change. (See Figure 2.3 for an overview of a change fund's key characteristics.) To start a change fund for athletic event ticket sales, for example, write a check from your checking account, coding it to a cash account titled "Change Fund—Athletics." Make the check equal to 15–20 percent of expected ticket sales, and be sure to obtain a variety of bills and coins. If there will be more than one ticket seller, you will need to divide the fund among all sellers.

Note, though, that access to cash provides an open opportunity for loss or misuse of school funds. The following guidelines will allow your school to protect the change fund while making it available for the intended purpose.

- Use a change fund *only* to make change; the money is not to be used to reimburse staff for school-related expenditures (University of Virginia, 2002). Never use a change fund to make loans to students and staff or to cash personal checks.

- A change fund is temporary and specific. Do not maintain a change fund in the office for staff to use.

- The change fund amount should remain constant for the duration of the fund (e.g., $10 for a middle school dance; $500 for a high school football game).

- Keep a change fund in a locked box/drawer with compartments for coins and bills; during ticket sales, the change box should be located in a restricted area, with access limited to the ticket seller.

- At the end of the ticket sales event, each ticket seller verifies the amount of his/her change fund before turning the money over to the coordinator.

- Rules for using a change fund may vary with each school district, but generally, a change fund used during an admission sales event (like a school play) is deposited back into the school's checking account on the first business day following the event. If a night deposit is made, a separate deposit slip is prepared for the total of all change funds.

FIGURE **2.3**

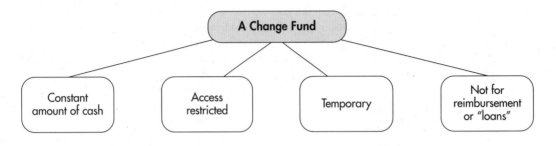

FORM **2-A**

Ticket Sales
Report
(see Appendix B, p. 127)

Reporting Admission Ticket Sales

Each ticket seller should complete a ticket sales report to reconcile the number of tickets personally sold with the amount of money personally collected. Ticket sellers should record basic information on the form before the ticket booth opens and complete the report immediately after the booth is closed. See Form 2-A for an example of a completed ticket sales report.

- Just prior to the event, the ticket seller records the colors and types of tickets to be sold (e.g., blue adult tickets, green student tickets, red child tickets, and the first ticket number available for sale in each ticket category (e.g. the first adult ticket number for sale is #505, the first student ticket for sale is #2000).

- When the ticket booth is closed, the ticket seller calculates* the number of tickets he/she has sold per ticket type. If the child tickets sold were numbered from 175 to 184, the number of tickets sold is 10 (i.e., tickets 175, 176, 177, 178, 179, 180, 181, 182, 183, and 184). An easy way to make this calculation is to write down the last ticket number sold plus one (1), then subtract the first ticket number sold. By adding "1" to 184 (the last ticket sold), the number of tickets sold can be determined by simple subtraction (i.e., 185 – 175 = 10 tickets sold).

- When the tallies are complete, the ticket seller calculates the funds collected for each ticket type (adult, student, child) by multiplying the cost of the ticket type by the number of tickets sold. The sum total of all ticket types should equal the total sales.

- Each ticket seller adds in the amount of his or her portion of the change fund on the ticket sales report and records the actual amount in the cash box/drawer.

- Finally, the ticket seller signs and dates the completed report and submits it to the event coordinator along with all funds. The ticket coordinator reviews all of the ticket sales reports and either turns the money in to the bookkeeper, who issues an office receipt, or makes a night deposit.

*If using a computerized form, this and other calculations will be automatic.

The Event Financial Report

The financial report is a summary document. It records the income from the event, as reported in individual ticket sales reports; summarizes all expenses related to the event; and verifies whether or not the event realized a profit or a loss. See Form 2-B for an example of a completed financial report.

- The event coordinator is responsible for completing the financial report. Insist that the report be completed promptly (within the week following an event).

- You, as principal, or a designated member of your administrative staff, should review the submitted financial report as soon as possible. If funds or tickets are missing, you will want to know right away.

Event Workers: Payment and Taxation Issues

Confusion often arises over whether or not an event worker is considered a "school employee" (who must be paid through the district's payroll office) or an independent, contracted service provider (who may be paid from a check drawn from activity funds).

➤ **Event Workers as "School Employees"**

Here is an overview of the Internal Revenue Service (2003a) guidelines for determining if an event worker should be considered a school employee. (See Figure 2.4 for a graphic summary.)

- If the person working at a school event is also an employee of the school district, the worker is considered an employee. Payments for working at events such as football games must be included in the employees' yearly wages (i.e., payments are added to the Form W-2). In other words, all earnings must be paid through the district's payroll office.

- If the person working at a school event is an employee of the same governmental jurisdiction (e.g., the City of Chicago; Oneida County, New York), the worker is considered a jurisdiction employee and must be paid through his or her regular payroll system. This includes employees who may work for a different agency within the same jurisdiction. Examples are city police officers that work for the city public schools as security officers during athletic events, the annual open house for parents, or other school programs.

- Finally, individuals who do not work as employees of the school system, but who offer paid services by working events under the direction of the school on a consistent, long-term basis (e.g., the secretary's husband works all basketball games as a ticket seller) are considered "school employees" and must be paid through the district's payroll office. According to the Internal Revenue Service (2003a, p. 5), these individuals are "school employees" if the school *provides instructions on how to do the work,* including (1) when, where, and what order to do the work; (2) what tools or equipment to use; (3) what workers to hire or assist with the work; (4) where to purchase supplies; and (5) what work must be performed by a specified individual.

| FORM **2-B**

Event Financial
Report
(see Appendix B, p. 127)

Never pay an event worker in cash. Cash payments to school employees, city employees, and game officials who work school events are likely to violate IRS rules regarding the payment of taxes. Check with your district's accounting department to ensure compliance.

FIGURE **2.4**

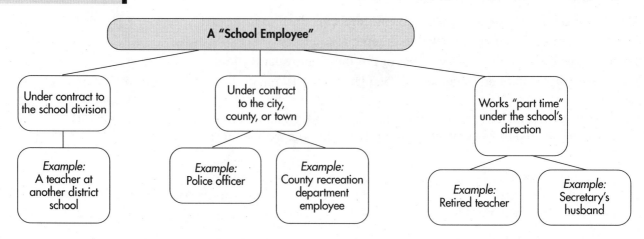

> ➤ **Event Workers as "Contracted Service Providers"**

- As a rule of thumb, workers are considered contracted service providers when a school explicitly contracts with a vendor for the services those workers provide (e.g., a security firm used to supply guards).

- The IRS's formal guideline is that workers are considered independent contractors if the school directs only the *outcome* of the work (e.g., independent trade professionals, such as a catering business or lawyers who offer their services generally to the public). The general rule is that an individual is an independent contractor if you, the payer, have the right to control or direct only the result of the work and not the means and methods of accomplishing the task" (Internal Revenue Service, 2003a, p. 3).

- Pay for these vendor-supplied services with school activity funds, issuing payment through a check written to the vendor. The school pays the vendor, and the vendor pays its contract employees.

- It is the vendor's responsibility to ensure that government regulations are followed (e.g., Fair Labor Standards, Workers' Compensation, payroll taxes).

For further information on event worker payroll and tax issues, contact your accounting department or visit the Internal Revenue Service Web site (http://www.irs.gov).

Summary

Adherence to controls and reporting requirements is essential when a school generates funds through the sale of admission tickets. Soon after the event, meet with the event coordinator (e.g., the athletic director, the school fair sponsor) to go over ticket sales reports and the financial report to determine if the event realized a profit and to confirm accurate accounting for the tickets sold and the tickets remaining. Solve any problems associated with ticket sales immediately and learn from the experience in order to eliminate future problems.

Remember to pay all "school employees" through the payroll office to avoid owing the federal government current and past payroll taxes. Your district accounting and internal audit departments will be glad to assist you if you have payroll questions.

tip

If you classify an employee as an independent contractor with no reasonable basis for doing so, the school may be liable for payroll taxes.

3

Bank Reconciliation

Bank Reconciliation—
The process of ensuring that items listed on the school's bank statements (i.e., checking and savings accounts) accurately represent the information recorded in the school's books. The purpose of preparing the bank reconciliation is to identify differences between the bank's balance and the school's financial records (e.g., bank service charges, interest earned) and to verify the reasons for the differences, based on written documentation.

The reconciliation of the school's bookkeeping records with the bank statements of the school's checking and savings accounts is one of the most important financial safeguards available to a principal. The process provides a regular snapshot of the accuracy and legitimacy of your school's financial records, and it is an important indication of how other financial tasks are being handled in your school on a daily basis. In other words, problems with the bank statement may signal financial problems elsewhere in your school's accounts. Repeated, irreconcilable differences between a bank statement and the school's books may indicate incompetence or fraud.

Bank Reconciliation Frequency

Bank reconciliation for the school checking account should be prepared each month, when the monthly bank statement arrives. Prompt attention is important, because banks typically require notification of fictitious checks (e.g., paying a bogus vendor) within 30 to 60 days in order to recover funds. Failure to notify a bank within this time frame could result in a permanent loss to the school (Thompson, 1999). Bank reconciliation for a school savings account should be prepared at least quarterly.

To ensure that you do not overlook these important review dates, insert a reminder in either your print or electronic calendar. We also recommend establishing an "in box" used exclusively for financial documents to ensure that these items are addressed quickly.

Bank Reconciliation Process and Format

The task of the individual preparing the bank reconciliation is to compare the bank statement with the school's books to ensure that all differences between the two have been identified. The bank reconciliation format may differ from school district to school district, but the following two-step format is the one that accountants use most often (Meigs & Meigs, 1992).

- The first step is to adjust the *bank statement balance* for transactions that the school has posted but the bank has not yet processed (e.g., deposits made on the last day of the month after banking hours, school checks that have not cleared the bank account).

- The second step is to adjust the school's *checking account balance* for the same period for transactions that the bank has posted, but the school has not yet recorded (e.g., interest earned, service charges).

- The adjusted bank balance from step 1 should equal the adjusted balance for the school's checking account in step 2 for the same period. See Form 3-A for a completed example of a standard bank reconciliation document.

- As a final step, sign and date the reconciliation form and have your book-keeper file it for audit review.

Responsibility for Bank Reconciliation

In many schools, the bookkeeper automatically reconciles the bank statement on behalf of the principal. For stronger internal control, we suggest that you ask someone *other* than the bookkeeper (e.g., an assistant principal, the general secretary) to perform this task. This separates the functions of receipting and disbursing funds from the reconciliation process, providing an extra safeguard.

Regardless of who prepares the bank reconciliation, you, the principal, should always review the reconciliation document—and your school's bank statements and financial statements—every month. Once you complete your review, sign and date the reconciliation document to indicate your approval and to ensure a clear audit trail.

The Principal's Bank Reconciliation Review

Here are important items to look for when reviewing the monthly bank reconciliation. (See Figure 3.1 for a graphic summary.)

- Review checks that cleared the bank for unusual items (e.g., checks without your signature, payments to unknown vendors).

- Review the deposits listed on the statement for gaps in the deposit dates (e.g., no deposits made during a week when a major fund-raising activity was held).

- Review the daily balance for both checking and savings accounts to ensure that neither exceeded $100,000—the maximum amount protected by the Federal Deposit Insurance Corporation (FDIC).

FORM 3-A

Bank Reconciliation
Form
(see Appendix B, p. 128)

Reconciliation is not complete until all reconciling items (e.g., outstanding checks, service charges) have been identified. There should never be a difference between the bank statement and school's books that cannot be explained by documentation.

- Review the beginning and ending balance of the school's bank account to ensure that the school is not in the red.

- Review the sequence of check numbers for gaps and to make sure that discontinued checks are not being used. Using blank checks from previous years is a common way of covering in-house theft.

- Review miscellaneous charges to ensure that they are reasonable (e.g., printing charges for additional checks, minimum balance service charge).

FIGURE 3.1

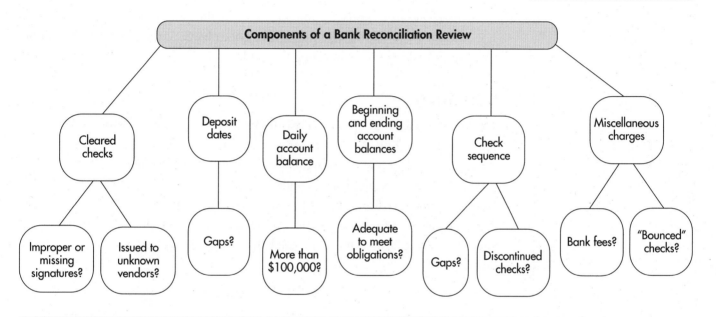

Components of a Bank Reconciliation Review

Common Bank Statement Items

The process of reconciliation accounts for the normal disparities between a routine bank statement and your school financial records. To facilitate your monthly reconciliation, here are the most common items that are likely to appear on a routine bank statement:

- *Outstanding checks* are checks issued by the school that have not yet cleared the school's checking account (e.g., a check issued on the last day of the month may not clear the bank until the next month).
- *Deposits in transit* are deposits added in the school's records that the bank has posted at a later date (e.g., end of the month receipts taken to the bank after 2:00 p.m. are posted to the next business day or the first day of the new month).
- *Service charges* are the bank's monthly fees for processing checks and deposits. A service charge may be based on the average daily balance in the bank account.
- *Nonsufficient funds (NSF)* are bank charges for the school's deposit of checks from individuals who lack sufficient funds to cover the payment.

(In other words, a check from a school patron "bounced.") In these instances, the bank will charge the deposit amount back to the school, along with a processing fee.

– *Interest earned* is based on the balance in the school's account. In most instances, the school does not know the amount until the monthly bank statement arrives; therefore, the interest is not posted to the school's records until the following month.

– *Miscellaneous bank charges* are fees for specially requested services that are not included in the monthly service charges (e.g., printing fees for deposit slips or checks).

– *Miscellaneous deposits* are adjustments that the bank may grant for various reasons (e.g., refunding a previous service charge, corrections for deposit or check cashing errors made by the bank).

Summary

The bank reconciliation process provides insight into the accuracy of your school's bookkeeping. A bookkeeper who struggles each month to explain why the bank statement and the school's bookkeeping records cannot be reconciled may be having other problems handling your books. Never omit a review and always require that discrepancies be explained with clear written documentation. The time you allot to the review of bank reconciliation is well worth the assurance of knowing that each month, the bank's records match the school's financial records.

4

Bookkeeping Basics

School Bookkeeping—
The tracking, through records, of funds going in and out of the school in support of school activities under the direct control of the principal. Bookkeeping records are maintained daily by a school bookkeeper, who is responsible for accuracy and diligent adherence to procedures applicable to all staff members who handle school funds. The principal bears direct responsibility for ensuring compliance with state and district accountability rules regarding school funds.

For many principals, the basics of school bookkeeping are shrouded in mystery, because of a lack of experience and training during their preparation for the principalship. Fortunately, the fundamental rules for bookkeeping can be learned at any time. Basic school bookkeeping principles and procedures are no more complex than the system for meeting your state accreditation standards and the required test score analysis for doing so. This chapter is intended to remove the mystique from the basic bookkeeping process (without attempting to make you the bookkeeper) and to provide you with the concepts and vocabulary you'll need to communicate with your bookkeeper and central office accountants with confident clarity.

An Overview of School Activity Funds

All of the money in your school is placed in one of many possible accounts, according to the school activity that it is intended to support, hence the name "school activity funds." For example, money collected for a field trip is placed in a field trip account; money from the sale of tickets for a senior play is placed in the drama club account; money set aside to cover the costs of mailing correspondence and bill payments is placed in the postage account. The funds in each account are then tracked throughout the school year as money is received and spent. On a day-to-day basis, bookkeeping tracks the money that comes into a school, sees that it is added to the appropriate activity fund account, and, when the time comes to spend money, sees that it is deducted from the appropriate activity fund account.

➤ The Types of Activity Fund Accounts

To ensure proper accounting for school activity funds, bookkeeping tracks the money in two ways: by *cash account* and by *fund account*. Together, cash accounts and fund accounts make up school activity funds under the internal control of a school principal (see Figure 4.1).

Cash Accounts

All school money is physically located in one of several *cash accounts*—your school's change funds, petty cash fund, checking account, and savings account. Tracking by cash account shows where school money is: in a change box for the school dance, in the petty cash box in the office, and in the bank.

Fund Accounts

School money is also categorized into *fund accounts* according to the money's origin and purpose. Tracking by fund account shows where the money came from; its intended purpose; and how, when, and by whom it is spent. Fund accounts are further subdivided into three basic types, according to the kind of activity they support financially:

– *School accounts* contain money used to operate the school and provide educational resources for the entire student body (e.g., general fund, English supplies). These funds may be allocated by the district, come from donations and grants, or come from whole-school fund-raising events or activities like the school store.
– *Student accounts* contain money raised by specific students groups (e.g., clubs, teams, grade levels) and used to benefit that group (e.g., when the student government sells bumper stickers, profits go into the student government account and are spent on student government needs).
– *Flow-through accounts* contain money that the school collects on behalf of the central office or another program (e.g., summer school funds). These funds are not available for your school budget and must be forwarded to the central office at the appropriate time.

tip

Remember that cash accounts must equal fund accounts.

FIGURE **4.1**

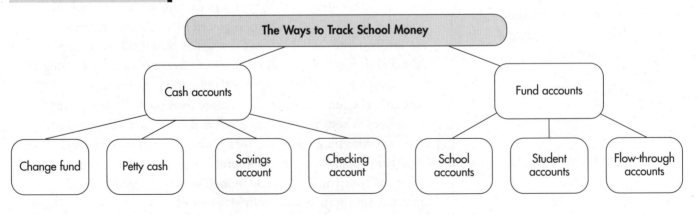

➤ **Special Characteristics of School Activity Funds**

Activity funds are unique public educational funds because, unlike district general operating funds, the principal authorizes the spending of this money at the school level on behalf of teachers and students.

All schools are allocated money from the district operating budget in one of several ways. This money is sometimes held by central office accounting in "draw accounts," where money is designated for individual schools, but is not deposited in checking accounts directly under the principals' control. District operating funds may also be allocated to schools in "reimbursement accounts," where schools make purchases first and then receive reimbursement from the district. In both of these allocation methods, the individual school and the central office track the expenditure of district operating funds, with the central office maintaining the official accounting records. However, if money is directly paid to an individual school by check, then that school bears sole responsibility for tracking expenditures through school activity funds. Regardless of allocation source or method, the principal is responsible for ensuring that funds are spent for the intended purpose, usually within one school year.

As principal, you need to be aware of activity funds' special characteristics.

- Activity funds are recorded and managed on a *cash basis of accounting,* which means that the money in these accounts is recorded at the time of receipt or payment. Purchases from activity funds are permissible only when the cash is available to cover the cost (Thompson & Wood, 1998).

- Activity funds can be spent in the current school year or a future school year (i.e., the funds do not have a spending time limit). Only funds that have a predetermined time limit (e.g., grant funds managed at the school, instructional funds allocated by the district) must be returned to the governing body that allocated the funds at the close of the allocation period. Unlike district operating funds (which normally must be reverted to the city or county government at the end of the school year if unspent), school activity funds raised by the school do not expire.

- Although activity funds can be carried over from year to year, they should be used to benefit the students who are in school at the time the funds were generated (Chicago Public Schools, 2002). For example, teachers should not increase the cost of a field trip so that a class will have extra funds in the field trip account for future years. As a general rule, look to spend at least 90 percent of the funds in an account during the year these funds are raised.

- Usually, state law requires that activity funds be audited annually. Even if an audit is not required, it is highly recommended to prevent undetected misuse and theft.

Basic Guidelines for Spending School Activity Funds

Before discussing bookkeeping procedures for activity funds, we need to cover the prudent guidelines for spending school activity funds (Virginia Department of Education, 1989). Follow these guidelines unless your district and state specifically allow exceptions to these principles in writing. The most important

tip

Spend district operating funds before you spend activity funds.

thing to remember about spending activity funds is that although you are the steward of activity funds, they are not yours to spend, lend, or borrow in any way that you see fit.

- Use school activity funds for the purpose for which these funds have been raised or allocated. In other words, do not redecorate the main office with funds intended for your instructional program.

- Use school activity funds raised by the entire student body to benefit all of your students. This guideline also applies to your general fund.

- Encourage student representation, with faculty supervision, in the management of funds raised by a student group.

- Spend activity funds on the students who were in school at the time the funds were raised. As mentioned, 90 percent is a good goal.

- Prohibit fund-raising projects that conflict with or detract from the instructional program or risk student safety (e.g., door-to-door sales).

- Manage school activity funds in accordance with sound budgetary and accounting procedures. Do not circumvent procedures mandated by your district and state.

- Ensure diligent record keeping and track activity fund spending on a regular, frequent basis.

Responsibilities for School Bookkeeping

As principal, you bear overall responsibility for your school's financial management. The overall supervision of your school's bookkeeping system is a responsibility you share with your district's central office. The central office accounting department may mandate many of the financial procedures and forms that your school uses, as well as the actual bookkeeping system. At the school level, it is your responsibility to make sure that your bookkeeper receives training in district procedures and the fundamental principles described in each chapter of this book. If your bookkeeper lacks training, request training from your district's accounting or internal audit office, or look for staff development opportunities that explain activity fund accounting procedures.

When you delegate financial administrative tasks (e.g., approving purchase orders or signing checks) during times when you are not available, make sure you assign the tasks to a responsible staff member. Also, carefully select faculty members to be in charge of fund-raising events and other school activities where money is received or spent. The buck always stops at the principal's office. If financial problems arise, the headache will be yours.

Basic Bookkeeping Principles

Supervising and communicating with your bookkeeper is much easier and much more effective when you understand a few basic bookkeeping principles.

- As mentioned on page 22, your bookkeeper tracks school funds by cash account and by fund account. The total of all the *cash accounts* must equal the total of all the *fund accounts*. Therefore, if your school has no petty cash fund, change fund, or savings account, but has $5,000 in a checking account, there must be $5,000 in the school's fund accounts. This $5,000 may be divided in a variety of ways among student accounts, school accounts, and flow-through accounts, but the total of all activity fund accounts must equal the total of all cash accounts. If your bookkeeping software captures *encumbrances* (money set aside for the purchase of goods or services prior to payment), your overall fund balance decreases by the amount of the encumbrances. The cash balance minus the balance of all encumbrances is the money that is uncommitted and available for spending.

- Each day, your bookkeeper *posts* (enters information) into the school's bookkeeping records. These entries produce various results. Each transaction increases, decreases, or does not change the total dollars available for spending. Figure 4.2 shows the various types of bookkeeping transactions and the effect each transaction-type has on a school's cash accounts and fund accounts.

tip

Issuing a purchase order increases the encumbrance balance, which decreases the amount available. Using an encumbrance system (see Chapter 7) helps you to avoid overspending activity funds.

FIGURE **4.2**

Transaction Effects on Cash Accounts and Fund Accounts

Type of Transaction	Effect on Cash Accounts	Effect on Fund Accounts
The bookkeeper issues an office receipt for money received.	Balance increases	Balance increases
The bookkeeper voids an office receipt.	Balance decreases	Balance decreases
The bookkeeper issues a check for a purchase.	Balance decreases	Balance decreases
The bookkeeper voids a check previously issued for the purchase of merchandise.	Balance increases	Balance increases
The bookkeeper transfers funds between different cash accounts (e.g., savings to checking).	No effect	No effect
The bookkeeper corrects an error in posting between two fund accounts (e.g., fund-raising and field trips).	No effect	No effect
The bookkeeper issues a purchase order.	No effect*	Fund balance decreases and encumbrance balance increase

* The purchase order reserves the cash; funds are not spent until a check is issued for payment.

- The bookkeeping process runs more smoothly when it adheres to a few simple rules:

  – All transactions (e.g., issuing school checks) must be supported by clear and accurate documentation (e.g., purchase orders, vendor invoices).

– Bookkeeping activity must be recorded each day (e.g., write daily receipts to teachers). Daily financial activity is summarized in a number of reports (e.g., cash receipts journal, bank deposit register), which are easily generated in most bookkeeping software packages. Examine these reports frequently to monitor daily financial activity. As principal, you should be generally familiar with these reports and the information they contain.

– Transactions that obligate funds (e.g., purchase orders) should be reviewed and approved before they occur. The issuance of a purchase order after an item is ordered or received is not acceptable accounting procedure!

– All staff members (e.g., bookkeeper, assistant principal, and teachers) must understand and adhere to school-mandated bookkeeping procedures.

• If you have questions about bookkeeping procedures, contact your district's accounting and auditing departments. Remember, they are there to assist you.

• Finally, we recommend that all principals regularly ask their bookkeeper a number of key financial questions, which we present in Appendix A.

The Components of the Bookkeeping Process

The bookkeeping process consists of a number of orderly procedures carried out to account accurately for the receiving and spending of funds in schools. The sections that follow explain the major components of this process.

➤ Accounting for Cash Receipts

Schools take in money every day, usually in small denominations, particularly at certain times of the year, such as the opening days of school. In bookkeeping terminology, this money is called "cash receipts," whether it is actual cash (bills and coins) or a check. There are a few basic steps your bookkeeper should follow to ensure accurate accounting for daily cash receipts.

• As teachers bring money and receipts to the office, your bookkeeper should count the money and total the amount for receipts issued as soon as possible. The total amount of cash and checks submitted to the office should match the total amount of the individual receipts issued by a teacher.

• At the time the dollar amount is entered in the bookkeeping system, your bookkeeper should issue the teacher an office receipt for that amount.

• Your bookkeeper should record office receipts issued to individual teachers in the *cash receipts journal.* (In a computerized bookkeeping system, this journal entry is automatic, and your bookkeeper needs only to review the entries for correctness.) The cash receipts journal is a summary report that lists by number the office receipts issued on a particular date. Usually, it also includes the name of the person who was issued the receipt (i.e., who brought money to the bookkeeper), the dollar amount of the receipt, and the activity fund account (e.g., school pictures, student government, athletic fund) that was increased.

• The cash receipts journal provides a means for comparing the individual receipts issued by teachers to the office receipts issued by your bookkeeper. It allows you, your bookkeeper, and visiting auditors to verify that funds were submitted to the office every day, and it helps the bookkeeper reconcile daily office receipts with daily bank deposits.

➤ Preparing Bank Deposits

- Ideally, your bookkeeper will prepare a daily bank deposit slip by listing the cash and checks received for the day. The total of the bank deposit should be compared to the total listed in the *bank deposit register* to make sure that the two figures match. A bank deposit register is simply the record of the amount to be deposited, based on the amount of money received that day. In most cases, the total of the cash receipts journal and the total of the daily deposit register are the same.

- The reason both a cash receipts journal and a deposit journal are important is that the cash receipts journal updates the school's financial records (e.g., your monthly financial report). The deposit register, on the other hand, updates that portion of the bookkeeping records that pertains to the monthly bank reconciliation process, showing all the deposits that are expected to appear on the bank statement. The two reports also allow for cash to be received on one day and deposited on a different day. This can be prudent when the collections for one day are recorded but are not deposited because the amount collected is very small—less than $25, for example. (In general, however, making daily deposits is a wise practice.)

- When the monthly bank statement arrives, you, the principal, should (1) review the deposits listed on the statement for gaps in the deposit dates (e.g., no deposits made during a week when a major fund-raising activity was held) and (2) compare the deposits listed to those in the school deposit register. For more information on reconciling your bank statement, see Chapter 3: Bank Reconciliation.

tip

Use the bank deposit register to help you reconcile your monthly bank statement with your monthly financial statement.

➤ Posting and Tracking Cash Disbursements

The handling of money going out is another of your bookkeeper's major responsibilities. Just as there is a logical set of procedures for safeguarding money received at your school, there is a logical set of procedures for making payments from school funds.

- Each time a payment is made from activity funds, the transaction should be posted to the *cash disbursements journal,* a (normally) computerized report that gives the date a check was written, the check number, the name of the person or company being paid, the dollar amount of the check, and the activity fund account that was reduced by the payment.

- The cash disbursements journal is organized by the dates checks were written, and it is used to ensure that checks were issued in numerical order and that no check is missing. It is also used to verify that payments by check are posted to the proper account code in the correct amount.

➤ Preparing Payment Packages

- As the bookkeeper processes payments, he or she will prepare *payment packages* for administrative review and approval. A payment package is a collection of all relevant documentation to justify writing a check from school funds.

- The payment package includes either a copy of the check or the computerized check stub; vendor invoices or original store receipts; the purchase order; and "receiving documents" from the merchandise packaging, in order to show that the item was actually received by the school.

- As the manager of school funds, examine checks in the payment package to make sure that the bookkeeper issued a check for all funds disbursed, then review each check to verify the following and ensure proper payment (see Figure 4.3 for a graphic summary):

  - The amount of the check matches the payment due. In the case of a check produced manually, make sure that the amount was entered into the computerized bookkeeping system correctly.
  - The check was issued to the same company or person approved on the purchase order.
  - The vendor's invoice or the store receipts are all original documents (i.e., no copies).
  - The purchase took place after the purchase order was approved (i.e., orders were not placed before you approved the purchase order).
  - The account from which the funds were drawn had a balance equal to or greater than the purchase amount (i.e., the activity fund account did not have a negative balance before or after the purchase).
  - The amount of the purchase was equal to or less than the amount that was approved, and the proper fund account was decreased by the expenditure.

FIGURE 4.3

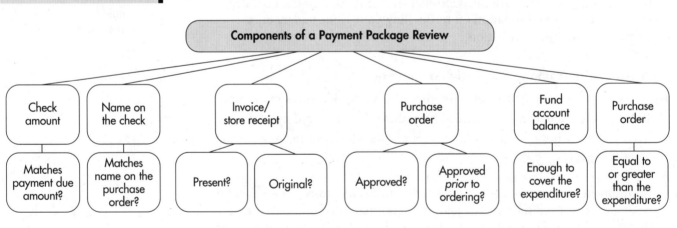

- As you approve payments, look for the following indicators of improper payment (see Figure 4.4 for a graphic summary):

  - Checks made payable to "Cash."
  - Unnumbered checks or checks written out of sequence.
  - Checks issued to staff members, individuals, or privately owned companies that are not incorporated for services provided. The IRS requires organizations to complete Form 1099-MISC when payments to individuals or private companies exceed $600 in any calendar year (Internal Revenue Service, 2002a). This guideline applies to payments issued by your school

district as a whole, not your school alone. Accordingly, you need to make a copy of all school checks payable to individuals or private companies and forward these copies to your district accounting office. This office will issue a Form 1099-MISC to each service provider for tax filing purposes.

– Checks with only one signature. All checks should have at least two signatures, one of which is yours! The purpose of multiple signatures is to confirm decisions about who to pay, when to pay, and how much to pay. For additional control, make the "second signer" someone other than your bookkeeper.

– Blank checks. Never sign—or approve—a blank check. Never! Signed blank checks are easily used for theft of school funds.

FIGURE **4.4**

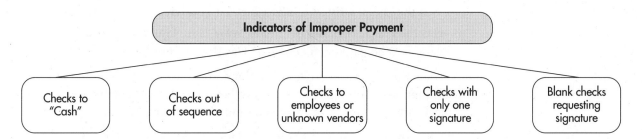

➤ **Issuing and Tracking Purchase Orders**

A school orders many items during the course of a year. As the principal, you need to establish purchase order procedures that ensure your school's compliance with procurement guidelines established by your state, city, county, or school board. Once the procedures are in place, the purchase orders are issued and recorded within your bookkeeping system in order to reserve money for payment.

• Most bookkeeping software packages have a purchase order module that will track the purchase orders from the time they are issued to the time vendors are paid. The purchasing section of the program will let you view "open" purchase orders (i.e., purchase orders that have been issued, but the items have not been paid for by the school).

• Another useful report in the purchasing module is the *purchase order status report*. This report includes summary information such as purchase order number, date of the order, the name of the person or company being issued the purchase order, the fund account that was charged with the encumbrance (i.e., the estimated amount of the purchase used to set aside funds), and the actual purchase order amount. Reviewing this document helps to ensure that the school has issued purchase orders in numerical order, that there are no missing numbers, that all purchase orders were approved by you, and that the fund account to be charged for the expenditure has an adequate balance. It also lets you verify actual payment to a vendor. During an audit, auditors usually review the purchase order status report, so it is a good idea for you to be familiar with it.

tip

Always ask for a copy of the purchase order status report.

➤ Reviewing Banking Information

Your banking records reveal a great deal about how your school handles financial matters. As a proactive principal, you should promptly review the monthly bank statements issued for your school's checking and savings accounts. Here are some suggested steps for reviewing each statement. (See Figure 4.5 for a graphic summary.)

- Review each cleared check, looking for any usual circumstances:

  - Were signature procedures followed? (For example, are there two signatures on each check? Has a staff member signed a check payable to himself or herself?)
  - Does the endorsement signature of the person or company who received the check match the name listed on the check?
  - Was the check written to a vendor that you have never heard of?
  - Has the check been altered in any way? (For example, has the name of the person to be paid been changed? Has the amount been changed?)

- Review the sequence of check numbers to make sure there are no large gaps and that discontinued checks are not being used. Using blank, discontinued checks from previous years is a common way of covering in-house theft.

- Review the beginning and ending balance of the school's bank account to ensure that the school is not in the red.

- Review the deposits processed by the bank to make sure that your school made deposits regularly and often (daily is preferred) and that the amount of all deposits equals the amount of receipts issued by your bookkeeper.

- Review the daily account balance to make sure that it did not exceed the $100,000 limit for insurance as established by Federal Deposit Insurance Corporation (FDIC). Balances in excess of $100,000 are not unusual for large high schools, and exceeding this limit is an unnecessary school risk.

- Review bank reconciliations and statement adjustments, looking for bank fees, service charges, errors made by the school in completing deposit slips, "stop payments" on checks, and checks from patrons that were returned due to nonsufficient funds (NSF). Do not accept that a bank reconciliation or statement adjustment is legitimate unless you know the facts (e.g., you have seen a returned check from a parent).

- For further information and detailed steps for reconciling your school's monthly bank statement, see Chapter 3: Bank Reconciliation.

FIGURE **4.5**

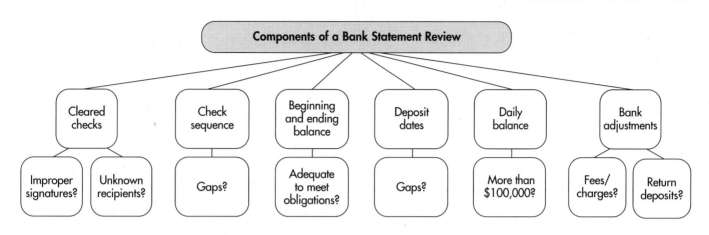

➤ Combining Accounts at the End of the Year

Major activity funds accounts are often divided into subaccounts to provide more detailed tracking during the school year. For example, you might divide the major field trip account into subaccounts by grade level or academic department for each field trip planned. At the end of the school year, your bookkeeper should combine all subaccounts back into the major activity fund account. This process allows you to start fresh each school year and to track the profitability of fundraising accounts more accurately. It's similar to reorganizing your closets in the spring so that you can see the clothing you really have.

Accounts to combine

The following are typical examples of subaccounts that a school will need to combine at the end of a school year. You may find this list helpful when it comes time to "close your books."

• If your general fund account is divided into separate budget accounts (e.g., minor school maintenance, copier, cell phones), close these accounts and transfer money back into your general fund in preparation for your next budget year. (See Chapter 15: School Budget, for information on preparing a projected budget.)

• As mentioned, if you are accounting for each field trip, have your book-keeper close these subaccounts into the main account for field trips by group (e.g., transfer funds from accounts such as "3rd Grade—Marine Science Museum" into the general field trip account for 3rd grade). This assumes of course, that no refunds are due to the students (see Chapter 8: Field Trips).

- If you are maintaining detailed accounts for each fund-raising event held by individual student groups, have your bookkeeper close these accounts into each group's main fund-raising account (e.g., transfer funds from "Cheerleaders—Car Wash" into the major account "Fund-Raising—Cheerleaders"; see also Chapter 9: Fund-Raising Events).

- In the same way, subaccounts for each athletic event should be transferred into the main account for athletics (e.g., close detailed accounts such as "Football Game—09/27/03" and transfer funds into the athletic fund account).

Accounts to keep separate

There are some accounts that should not be combined at year-end. The overriding principle is not to commingle funds intended for one group with the funds intended for another group. Remember, you should always use activity funds for the purpose intended and for the group intended.

- Do not combine accounts that belong to different student groups (e.g., the fund-raising account of one grade with the fund-raising account of another grade).

- Do not combine accounts where the central office requires detailed reporting (e.g., summer school money with "lost or damaged textbook" fees).

- Do not combine accounts that are from different fund sources (e.g., funds for the student government into a school account such as the general fund).

Summary

Mastering the basics of school bookkeeping is an essential skill set for the principalship. Still, many new principals enter the position well prepared for all aspects of the job *except* this one. Because failure in the management of school funds can be both stressful and potentially harmful to a principal's long-term career, many principals abdicate this important responsibility almost entirely to the school bookkeeper, who may or may not be sufficiently trained and trustworthy to handle the job.

Fortunately, the basics of bookkeeping can be learned at any time, and by even the busiest principals. By understanding the important principles and procedures for receiving and spending money for typical events that occur in all schools, you will increase your confidence and competence as an administrator. Remember, too, that proper bookkeeping also streamlines the managerial aspect of your job so that you can concentrate your efforts on where they belong: on your students, parents, and staff.

5

Credit/Purchasing Cards

School Credit/Purchasing Cards—*Credit cards obtained in the name of an administrator, school, or district for the purpose of charging school purchases or vendor-provided travel services. The principal's prior approval and the close monitoring of charged expenses are essential procedures to reduce the likelihood of fraudulent, improper, and questionable purchases.*

The use of school purchasing or credit cards has increased in recent years, reflecting an attempt to reduce the paperwork associated with small purchases and travel expenses. These cards are similar to a personal credit/debit card, but with two big differences: (1) school districts and schools usually restrict card use to certain kinds of expenses (e.g., only instructional supply purchases), and (2) no personal expenses are permitted.

This chapter outlines the basic procedures to establish at your school so that you and your staff can take advantage of the convenience purchasing cards offer while avoiding unwise or fraudulent use. If you set up good procedures and follow them strictly, purchasing cards can save your staff time and reduce the wait for needed materials and services.

Guidelines Governing Authorization to Use Purchasing Cards

There are several types of purchasing cards. The first type is issued to a department within the district (e.g., transportation, instruction) or to a particular school. (Some banks are now hesitant to issue cards to generic organizational groups.) The second type of card is issued to an individual employee. In either of these cases, the authority to use purchasing cards should be granted in writing from the district's administrator in charge of purchasing (e.g., the assistant superintendent or director of purchasing). Typically, this official grants a principal permission to acquire a district-approved purchasing card from a major company (e.g., VISA, MasterCard) that offers the most cost-effective card (e.g., no annual fee) and other incentives, such as printing a school's tax exempt number on the card. The third type of purchasing card is a vendor-specific card, to be used only at designated stores (e.g., Best Buy, Office Depot). Vendor-dedicated cards are less likely to be misused (e.g., no cash advances are possible). Regardless of the card type, the principal is responsible for overseeing its use at the school.

Determining Who Can Use a School Purchasing Card

Not all staff members need access to a purchasing card. Typically, only those staff members who normally purchase items on the school's behalf (e.g., sponsors, coaches, selected classroom teachers) should be designated as users. There are several other factors to consider when deciding who on your staff should be issued or have access to a purchasing card. Key questions to ask concerning potential users are listed here (University of Florida, 2000). See Figure 5.1 for a graphic summary of these points.

tip

Do not assume that staff members will automatically use proper purchasing card procedures. Training takes little time and is a valuable investment.

– Is the individual a full-time employee? Limit card use to full-time employees. Part-time staff (e.g., substitute teachers) could leave at any moment—you don't want them taking your purchasing card with them when they go.
– Does the staff member handle other school financial matters with "due diligence" (e.g., issues receipts properly, turns in collected money on time)? Restrict use to staff members with conscientious financial management skills.
– Has the employee received "training" on the use of the card (e.g., no personal expenditures, proper security, disposition of receipts) as indicated by a signed copy of a card user agreement form? Annual training is a major deterrent of problems.
– Is the employee in good standing with regard to future employment (e.g., there are no pending personnel actions)? Sudden dismissal could result in the loss or misuse of your purchasing card.
– Are there limits on where the card can be used (e.g., a vendor-specific card)? If so, does it make sense for the staff member to use the card, based on current job responsibilities?

FIGURE **5.1**

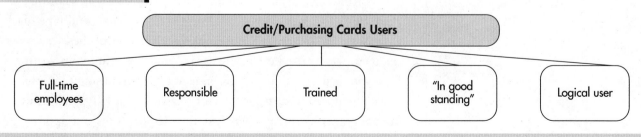

Prohibited Purchasing Card Expenditures

As a rule of thumb, if a purchase is not allowable with general school funds, it is not allowable with a purchasing card. Nonetheless, it may be helpful to review the following list of prohibited expenses (see Figure 5.2 for a graphic summary):

- Personal expenses (e.g., gasoline, groceries, furniture, software, clothing, or personal services).
- Cash advances from the credit card company.
- Nonrefundable items (e.g., custom-built furniture or signs).
- Hazardous materials (e.g., cleaning chemicals or lab chemicals) that require other documentation to be on file at the school (i.e., Material Safety Data Sheet in case of accident). Items governed by safety regulations are usually ordered by an authorized district administrator and distributed to individual schools.
- Items intended to be gifts or awards. These may appear to be personal purchases.
- Unapproved expenses, such as for items that require a central office purchase order (e.g., computers, telephones) or items that are not allowable expenditures (e.g., liquor).

• Your school district's policies and procedures dictate if a purchasing card may be used for travel-related expenses *and* the dollar limit for any single purchase (e.g., no purchase of individual items or a combination of items over $100). If travel expenses (e.g., airline tickets, hotel costs, meals) are allowed, an approved travel authorization form should be on file *before* the travel occurs (see Chapter 17: Staff Reimbursement).

• Make sure your school's procedures governing card use address the action (e.g., withdrawal of the card and/or personnel action) that will be taken against a card user for usage violations.

FIGURE **5.2**

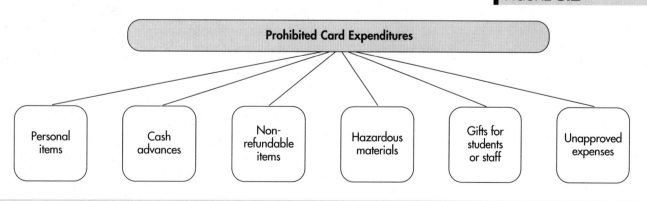

tip

Protect purchasing cards with the same security measures that you use to safeguard cash in the school.

Purchasing Card Responsibilities

Responsibilities pertaining to purchasing card distribution, verification, and storage are best divided among staff members (Stanford University, 2002).

➤ The Card Custodian's Responsibilities

- The card custodian is the person to whom the card is actually issued (e.g., an assistant principal). This person is responsible for controlling the card's distribution to designated individuals, tracking the use and location of the card, and ensuring that the card is kept in a secure location (e.g., the school safe).

- The card custodian communicates the rules for card usage and obtains a signed copy of a card user agreement form from all card users.

- The card custodian conducts an independent review of the monthly purchase card bills as they are received. Multiple reviews of monthly billing statements (one by the bookkeeper, another by the card custodian) help ensure appropriate card usage.

➤ The Card User's Responsibilities

- A card user is responsible for using a card for authorized school-related business only.

- A card user never lends or shares the card. The card user receives the card from the card custodian and, once a purchase is made, returns the card promptly. It's the card custodian's responsibility to distribute the card to other approved users.

- Before payment of the monthly expenses, each card user reviews and signs the monthly billing statement indicating that the charges to the card are correct and that the purchases were for authorized school merchandise or services.

  - The card user, not the bookkeeper, is responsible for identifying and disputing unauthorized charges (i.e., mistakes or errors on the part of the vendor or card user).

  - If a monthly statement includes unauthorized purchases not attributable to vendor error, the card user issues immediate payment to school.

- A card user never splits purchase transactions in order to circumvent the allowable dollar limit for card transactions.

- At the time of purchase, the card user requests that sales and use taxes not be charged, based on the school's tax exempt status as a nonprofit organization.

- After a purchase, the card user obtains, signs, and forwards the card receipts to the bookkeeper within three school days.

- The card user immediately reports a lost or stolen card to the credit card company who issued the card and to the principal.

➤ The Bookkeeper's Responsibilities

- The bookkeeper processes card receipts turned in by card users by recording the expenses in the bookkeeping system to encumber (i.e., obligate) funds in the appropriate accounts.

- The bookkeeper matches receipts from the card user to the purchases listed on the monthly statement from the credit card company.

- The bookkeeper reviews each card user's transactions for unauthorized purchases and verifies that all card users have signed the bill as an indication that the purchases were for school-related items.

- When card users submit payment for unauthorized purchases, the bookkeeper issues a school receipt to the card user indicating that the school has received reimbursement.

- Once all verifications of the billing statement are complete, the bookkeeper prepares the monthly payment check to the credit card company for the principal's approval.

➤ The Principal's Responsibilities

- The principal identifies and approves those staff members who can be card custodians or users.

- The principal authorizes the dollar limit for card purchases. Authorization can be in the form of a blanket purchase order in the vendor's name, stating that purchases are not to exceed a designated amount (e.g., $100). (See Form 5-A for an example.)

- The principal conducts the final review of the monthly billing statement, confirming that all transactions are appropriate and approving the actual payment of purchases charged to the card.

- The principal approves the monthly payment by check to the credit card company.

- The principal is the point of contact should the credit card company need to get in touch with a school employee regarding a bill or transaction (e.g., payment of the monthly bill was late).

- The principal is responsible for notifying the card issuer in writing if the card is lost or stolen. For this reason, it is important to have a record of the card number and the name on the card. Make a photocopy of the card and store it in your safe.

Lost or Stolen Purchasing Cards

In the subsections following, we provide procedures for reporting a lost card, outline liability issues, and present a series of precautions you can take to lower the risk of card loss or theft.

➤ Procedures for Reporting Loss

The Federal Trade Commission (2002) recommends that the following steps be taken when a credit/purchasing card is lost or stolen:

  – As soon as possible, report the loss or theft to the credit card company (e.g., VISA). Many companies maintain toll-free numbers and 24-hour service to deal with loss and theft emergencies.

  – Once the loss is reported, follow up the phone call with a letter. Be sure to include your account number, when you realized your school's card was missing, and the date you first reported the loss.

FORM **5-A**

Blanket Purchase
Order (Credit/
Purchasing
Card Use)
(see Appendix B, p. 129)

*Make sure all
reviews of the
monthly
statement are
complete before
you authorize
payment.*

It may also be wise to notify your district's purchasing and accounting offices of the card loss. They may be able to assist you in dealing with the issuing company and affected vendors. See Figure 5.3 for a graphic summary of these points.

FIGURE **5.3**

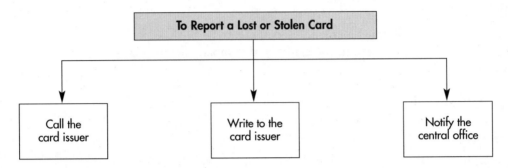

➤ Liability Issues

- Fortunately, the federal Fair Credit Billing Act (FCBA) limits the maximum liability your school (or any credit card holder) must bear for unauthorized charges made on a lost or stolen card. According to the Federal Trade Commission (2002)

  - If a thief uses your card before you report it missing, the most your school will owe for unauthorized charges is $50 per card.
  - If you report the loss or theft before the card is used, or if the loss involves only your credit card number (not the card itself), the credit card company cannot hold you responsible for *any* unauthorized charges.

- Stress to card users that prompt reporting of card loss or theft can absolve your school of all liability. Although waiting to notify the card issuer will not make your school responsible for endless unauthorized expenses, it may require you to spend valuable time on the telephone with the credit card company correcting those charges.

➤ Card Security Precautions

- Know where your purchasing card is, and keep it under lock and key.
- Open monthly statements immediately.
- Retain and file card receipts, and match each one to the billing statement.
- Make sure a company is reputable before you give your card number over the phone.
- Do not allow staff to write the card number on scrap paper and carry it with them.
- Cut up old cards before discarding them.
- Keep a record of your card number and the telephone number of the issuing company in a secure location.

Risks to Consider

Unauthorized use of purchasing cards is the major risk, and it can easily occur if recommended safeguards are not followed carefully. Reported purchasing card fraud is occurring in private industry (Keys, 1999) and government agencies ("Fraud," 2002) amounting to a loss of both funds and equipment. A 2002 U.S. General Accounting Office report on improper use of government purchasing cards in several federal agencies identified the main causes as inadequate adherence to written approval and review procedures for purchasing card transactions and insufficient training on those procedures. This lax environment allowed card users to make "fraudulent, improper, abusive, and questionable purchases" (U.S. General Accounting Office, 2002, p. 3).

The lesson is clear. Procedures are only useful when staff know them and follow them carefully. If you are not a methodical principal when it comes to school money matters, we suggest that you do not use purchasing cards at your school.

Summary

School purchasing or credit cards are a convenient buying tool for staff and are becoming increasingly popular because of the ease of use with vendors and the elimination of paper work associated with individual purchase orders. At the same time, the opportunity for mishandling and misuse of cards is great if you do not insist that all members of your staff adhere strictly to prudent procedures. As the principal, you must know the steps for approval and review and follow them carefully. Otherwise, you are better served by more traditional methods of obtaining and paying for the goods and services your school needs.

tip

Electronic ticket boxes operate like a cash register by recording the money collected and issuing the purchaser a prenumbered ticket or receipt.

6

Employee Embezzlement

School administrators sometimes have difficulty facing the possibility of employee theft because it is so foreign to the mission of schools and to the generally positive atmosphere characteristic of learning environments. Schooling is big business, however, and theft by school employees at all levels is on the rise (Walsh-Sarnecki, Schaeffer, & Ross, 2000). Consider, for example, that a typical high school may handle as much as $500,000 in any given year. Most of the money comes into the school in small-dollar amounts.

The accounting safeguards discussed in each chapter of this book, if implemented, can substantially reduce the risk of misuse or theft of funds. What's more, your awareness of the common ways that employee theft occurs can do much to prevent it from happening in your building.

The Facts on Employee Embezzlement

The embezzlement facts listed here were assembled by the Denver District Attorney's Office (2001) and are presented to help raise your awareness of how risky it is to rely too much on any one staff member when it comes to school financial matters:

- Embezzlement is an inside job, committed by a trusted staff member.
- Embezzlers know the school business and exploit their knowledge for illegal gain.
- Economic crime is a crime of premeditated calculation.
- Embezzlers are rarely reported to the police; statistically it pays to commit "white collar" crime.
- Offenders usually steal again.

Typical Embezzlement Strategies

Embezzlers use a variety of fairly standard strategies to steal school funds. Some of these strategies pertain to money received; others involve fraudulent payment activities. The most common practices among school embezzlers are described in the sections that follow.

➤ Fraudulent Receipt Activity

Schools are particularly vulnerable when only one bookkeeper handles office transactions related to incoming funds. Common theft strategies pertaining to money received at a school include the following:

- Collecting cash and not issuing a receipt.
- Omitting a receipt date so that the receipt cannot be traced to a particular deposit.
- Using a "hidden" receipt book to issue some receipts and stealing the cash associated with those receipts.
- Not issuing a receipt for money received by check and removing an equivalent amount from a cash drawer.
- Receipting money in the morning and restoring bookkeeping files from the previous day in order to cover theft through altered records.
- Swapping current personal checks for cash received to maintain the correct deposit amount and then delaying the deposit (Robertson, 2000).
- "Lapping," which is treating funds collected today as the receipts for a prior period (e.g., yesterday, a day last week). Essentially, the embezzler is using the school's money as a loan. An example of lapping would be Mrs. Smith collecting field trip money on Monday from her first period class and then "borrowing" that money for personal use. On Wednesday, she collects field-trip money from her second period class, and then turns in Monday's student receipts on Wednesday, along with the money collected on Wednesday. She repeats this process until she pays back the loan or just keeps the student funds in an attempt to cover the theft.
- "Kiting," which is posting bookkeeping transactions to conceal theft. An example would be the bookkeeper transferring money from the school's savings account to the school's checking account to conceal the theft of general fund money. Instead of posting this transaction as a transfer between two bank accounts, it is posted as an increase to the checking account and an increase to the general fund account. A decrease in the savings and general fund accounts is usually posted after the principal has reviewed the general fund balance, which appears correct.

➤ Fraudulent Payment Activity

Check-writing practices are easily subject to dishonest uses, including the following:

- Making payments to phony vendors (Wells, 2002a).
- Paying invoices more than once and then pocketing the refund when a company issues a check for overpayment (Wells, 2002b).

- Holding vendor payments to cover cash taken.
- Using school credit/purchasing cards to pay for personal items or obtain cash advances ("Fraud," 2002).
- Making checks payable to "Cash."

➤ Other Practices Associated with Fraud

A number of other fraudulent practices may occur among professional staff (Wells, 2001) if you are not careful to establish safeguards ahead of time:

- *Family fraud.* Beware of collusion among members of the same family when each is handling school money. If your bookkeeper is married to the fund-raising chairman, athletic director of the school, or PTA treasurer, suggest to the family members that this situation may present the appearance of impropriety. Encourage one of the family members to serve in a role that does not involve the handling of school or PTA funds.
- *Professional staff fraud.* Watch for inflated requests for reimbursements of supply and travel expenses. Also, be on the look out for reimbursement requests that are submitted more than once. If your school uses credit/purchasing cards, always review monthly statements carefully before authorizing payment (see Chapter 5: Credit/Purchasing Cards).

Never allow one family member to receipt money from another.

Your School's Vulnerability to Embezzlement

It's easy to underestimate a school's vulnerability to inside theft. The unfortunate truth is that, given opportunity and need, many school employees will "borrow" funds. It's also true that many traits of a really good bookkeeper are also the characteristics of a clever embezzler (see Figure 6.1). In short, do not expect to be able to "tell" embezzlers by the way they look, act, or dress. Successful ones are often "ideal employees" who are never absent, arrive early, and stay late (O'Rourke, 1998).

FIGURE **6.1**

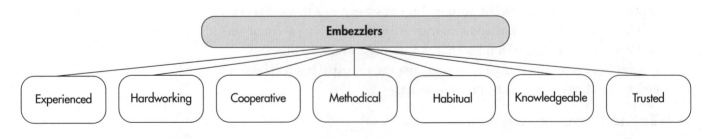

Take the quiz in Figure 6.2 to help assess your school's current vulnerability to employee theft.

Directions: For each question, circle the response that best describes your school's procedures.

1. How many employees handle the daily bookkeeping responsibilities?

   a. One

   b. Two, and bookkeeping functions are separated

   c. Three, and no one person is handling all bookkeeping duties

2. How many administrators at the school review the bookkeeping responsibilities?

   a. There is no administrative review of bookkeeping

   b. One

   c. Two

3. When money is received at the school, does someone other than the bookkeeper receipt the money and forward it to the bookkeeper?

   a. No, receipts are issued by the bookkeeper

   b. Yes, but there are times when the bookkeeper handles the entire process

   c. Yes, always

4. Does the bookkeeping staff take at least one week of vacation each school year?

   a. No

   b. Usually

   c. Yes, it is required

5. Does the same staff member issue receipts and make bank deposits?

   a. Yes, always

   b. Yes, most of the time

   c. No, these functions are separated

6. As the principal, do you periodically check the detail work of the bookkeeping staff?

   a. No, never

   b. Yes, but I am unsure of which items to compare and how to locate discrepancies

   c. Yes, and I know which items to check for discrepancies

7. Before hiring a bookkeeper, do you ensure that the employee's references and criminal background have been checked?

   a. No

   b. No, but I rely on the department of personnel, which performs the verification

   c. Yes, I review all the records of applicants after the department of personnel

(continued on next page)

FIGURE 6.2

School Embezzlement Vulnerability Quiz

Adapted with permission of the Denver District Attorney's Office from "What You Need to Know About Employee Embezzlement," available at http://www.denverda.org.

FIGURE **6.2**

School
Embezzlement
Vulnerability Quiz
(Continued)

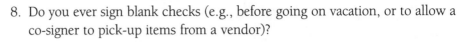

8. Do you ever sign blank checks (e.g., before going on vacation, or to allow a co-signer to pick-up items from a vendor)?

   a. Yes

   3   b. Yes, but I verify that the check amount equals documentation (e.g., check and invoice amount are the same)

   c. No, never

9. Are your office staff members cross-trained to perform bookkeeping duties?

   1   a. No

   b. Yes, somewhat

   c. Yes

10. Does the same employee handle bank deposit preparation and reconciling the monthly bank statement?

   1   a. Yes, always

   b. Yes, most of the time

   c. No, these functions are separated

11. Does your school division issue a written set of standard bookkeeping procedures?

   3   a. No

   b. We rely on a few important memos

   c. Yes, we follow a standardized procedures manual

12. Does an independent accountant conduct a detailed, annual audit of your school's books?

   a. No, but I submit monthly financial statements

   3   b. My school is audited, but not every year

   c. Yes, my school is audited at least once a year

13. Who prepares the bank reconciliation?

   a. The bookkeeper

   2   b. The bookkeeper prepares it, and as principal, I review and sign it.

   c. Someone with no bookkeeping duties prepares it, and as the principal, I review and sign it.

14. When the bookkeeper is away for five or more days, does another member of the office staff perform the bookkeeping duties?

   a. No, we hold the work until the bookkeeper returns

   b. Sometimes, but other staff members are not that familiar with "the books"

   c. Yes, another employee is trained to perform the bookkeeping duties

15. Does your school district offer bookkeeping training on school time?

   a. No

   b. Yes, every couple of years

   c. Yes, high quality training if offered every year

(continued on next page)

FIGURE 6.2

School
Embezzlement
Vulnerability Quiz
(Continued)

16. Is your bookkeeper covered by an employee fidelity bond policy?

    a. No

    b. Yes, but I do not review the amount of coverage

    c. Yes, and I verify the amount of coverage each year

Scoring: Give yourself 1 point for each *a* answer, 2 points for each *b* answer, and 3 points for each *c* answer.

Vulnerability Scale:

20 or fewer points	*Very Vulnerable.* The financial controls in your school are not sufficient to prevent embezzlement.
21–39 points	*Vulnerable.* Some controls are in place, but these controls need to be reviewed and increased.
40–48 points	*Not Very Vulnerable.* Most financial controls are in place to deter embezzlement.

Preventing Employee Embezzlement

Here are a few steps you can take to prevent embezzlement in your school.

- Welcome unannounced internal audits initiated by the district office, particularly when the same person is receiving and depositing money in your office.

- Insist that all requests for funds be made in writing.

- Be aware that an employee may be living well above his or her means. Discourage such a staff member from handling school money. If this person is your bookkeeper, be extra vigilant regarding appropriate financial procedures.

- Follow this book's advice for monitoring money coming in and going out of your school (see Chapter 1: Activity Fund Safeguards).

- Ask school auditors or accountants for advice when you are in doubt about appropriate accounting procedures or how to proceed on a suspicion regarding embezzlement.

Summary

Opportunity coupled with financial need is a dangerous combination that could adversely affect your career, the careers of your staff, and the reputation of your school. Heed the warning signs given in this chapter and avoid relying too much on any one staff member when it comes to financial management. Require and enforce the safeguards described in other chapters of this book to reduce your vulnerability to loss of funds from fraud or theft. It really is better to be safe than sorry.

7

Encumbrance of Funds

Encumbrance—

The amount of money that has been obligated by a purchase order or similar document before checks have been issued for payment. In an encumbrance system, a bookkeeping entry records the estimated cost of a purchase at the time that a purchase order is issued. These funds are adjusted when the actual invoice is received, but are still considered "expended" and unavailable for other purchases or payments (Fisher, Taylor, & Leer, 1982).

Making sure that school accounts are not overspent is one of a principal's major financial responsibilities. Typically, a school purchase is processed with a purchase order, and the bill is received at a later date. Once the purchase order is submitted, though, that money should be considered no longer available for other uses. In bookkeeping terms, this in an *encumbrance*—an estimated financial obligation.

Accounting for this obligated money can create many headaches if it is not done systematically. Follow the guidelines in this chapter to make the tracking of encumbrances a routine part of spending school funds and, thus, *avoid* surprise bills for purchases you forgot were underway!

Why You Should Track Encumbrances

Tracking encumbrances is the only way to be sure that money is not "spent" more than once. In the typical school, it is virtually impossible to remember all of the purchase orders that have been issued in all accounts and the amount of each. An encumbrance system sets aside the estimated cost of each purchase to ensure that funds are available when the actual bill becomes due.

- Use encumbrances to provide current information on available funds for planning purposes (e.g., how much money is available for spending in the spring?).

- Track encumbrances for "open" purchase orders to avoid overspending accounts (i.e., running an account in the red).

- Remember, tracking encumbrances is similar to tracking your personal credit card charges. If you do not keep track of the charges at the time of purchase, you may overspend your budget.

- Tracking encumbrances can also prevent you from underspending an account. The goal is to spend school funds for the intended purpose in the current school year. Returning unspent district funds to the central office year after year sends the message that your school is overfunded.

Assigning Responsibility for Tracking Encumbrances

It is logical for the bookkeeper to track encumbrances as part of the accounting process. Recording encumbrances should be a regular part of the purchasing process, and the bookkeeper's involvement is essential in purchase order review and processing so that all encumbrances are entered into the tracking system promptly.

Establishing an Encumbrance Tracking System

Establishing a system to encumber funds is not difficult. Basically, when a purchase order is approved and processed, a bookkeeping entry records the estimated cost of the financial commitment. When the invoice for the purchased items or services is received, the original entry amount is adjusted to record the actual cost of the item, including any additional expenses, such as delivery charges.

Here are various ways to set up an encumbrance system (see Figure 7.1 for a graphic summary):

- Use bookkeeping software (e.g., Manatee), if available, that includes a feature for tracking encumbrances.
- Use spreadsheet programs (e.g., Excel) to track open purchase orders (i.e., purchase orders that have not been paid).
- Use manual recordkeeping (i.e., the bookkeeper tracks encumbrances with a manual worksheet).

FIGURE **7.1**

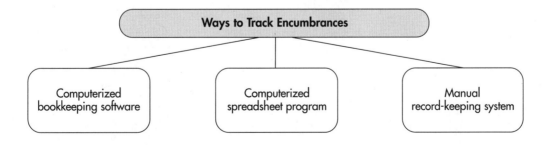

FORM **7-A**

Encumbrance
Tracking
Spreadsheet
(see Appendix B, p. 129)

Regardless of the encumbrance tracking system you use, the process is the same: the amount of a purchase order is subtracted from the current fund balance until the actual vendor's invoice is received, at which point the fund balance is adjusted to reflect any difference between the purchase order amount and the amount on the invoice. See Form 7-A for a sample encumbrance spreadsheet, which can be either manual or computerized.

Summary

An encumbrance system is an effective financial tool for a busy principal and office staff. It routinely deducts money from the correct account *when* purchase orders or contracts are approved and processed and *before* the corresponding bills are received. That way, funds are obligated immediately. You can also use the process to reserve funds for projects later in the school year with temporary, in-house purchase orders, specifying the needed amount to ensure that money is available at the appropriate time. Also, remember to review the status of all accounts with your bookkeeper at least quarterly in order to avoid overspending or underspending any one account.

8

Field Trips

Field Trips—
School-sponsored student trips that are directly related to the curriculum and planned by faculty members with the principal's permission and oversight. The costs of trips are paid for either by parents, profits from fund-raising events, or the school's general fund.

Field trips are a valuable part of the educational process and, when coordinated with the curriculum and carefully planned, a logical extension of the classroom. Because field trips involve costs, financial planning becomes very important. Typically, parents bear at least part of the cost for field trips, and if the group is large, money coming into the school for this purpose can be substantial. On the other hand, bills related to the trip, such as those covering transportation, admissions, and meals, can also be considerable.

This chapter explains the necessary financial steps for planning and conducting field trips and provides a sample permission form and a checklist to assist you with organizing a successful educational experience for students, parents, and staff.

School-Sponsored Trips vs. Private Trips

The type of school-sponsored, educational trip addressed in this chapter is to be distinguished from trips organized by individual staff members during vacations (e.g., a summer trip to France) or funded independently by parent organizations (e.g., a band trip to Disney World). Recreational trips of this type should not be planned, advertised, or financially accounted for on school property by school staff unless you are prepared to bear the legal responsibility for the safety of students while on such trips. Any trip *assumed* to be school-sponsored makes the school legally liable for student safety. For information on the legal aspects of nonschool-sponsored field trips, refer to the *American School Board Journal* online archive at http://www.asbj.com/.html.

Use the Internet to look up your school district's purchasing manual and state procurement regulations.

Purchasing Procedures for Field Trip Expenditures

Before signing a contract with a service provider such as a bus company, consider the dollar amount of the contract and what procedures are necessary to avoid violating state purchasing laws and district guidelines. Exceeding the allowable dollar limit set by some state purchasing laws can result in a principal's dismissal.

- Confirm the appropriate purchasing method for obtaining travel services. There are three questions to answer:

  – Is a formal bid required?
  – Is a price quote required?
  – Is a purchase order or written contract sufficient?

- Prohibit teachers from entering into financial contracts with service providers. Teachers do not bear the legal and financial responsibility for the school. Only an authorized school administrator should enter into contracts with travel service companies. Ask teachers to bring all contracts to you for your review, approval, and signature.

Selecting a Travel Service Vendor

Take the time to compare travel service providers before entering into a contract, particularly if you are new to the school or area. Safety issues are always the primary concern, but general reliability is a factor as well. Here are some guidelines for evaluating and selecting the best travel service vendor (see Figure 8.1 for a graphic summary):

– Review the vendor's past performance (e.g., does the vendor have a record of offering safe, dependable service? does the vendor employ responsible drivers without prior traffic violations or criminal records?).
– Determine what service the vendor will provide (e.g., the vendor agrees to pick up and return students to school).
– Confirm the vendor's policy regarding cancellation of a trip due to major weather problems or other extenuating circumstances, such as safety/security-related cancellations.
– Confirm the vendor's procedure for refunds if there are students who do not attend (e.g., students are sick the day of the field trip).

FIGURE **8.1**

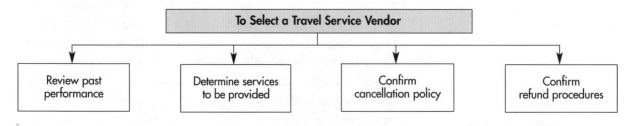

Field Trip Responsibilities

Responsibilities for a field trip are shared between you, the principal, and the faculty members organizing the trip. This section lists and explains the responsibilities of the principal (or another designated administrator, such as assistant principal) and the teaching staff (the trip sponsors) before and after a field trip. Make sure that all the tasks are assigned to conscientious staff members.

➤ **Principal's Duties Before the Trip**

– Designate the sponsors who are to handle the event and ask for justification linking the trip to the tested curriculum.

– Review the legal aspects of the trip, including school board policies and procedures. Be sure to adhere to policies that limit the number of field trips per grade or course.

– Authorize the trip in writing, and meet with trip sponsors to review their duties before, during, and after the field trip, paying particular attention to district procedures for receipting and depositing funds, and for vendor evaluation.

– Review, approve, and finalize any necessary vendor contracts.

➤ **Sponsors' Duties Before the Trip**

Before a field trip, the sponsors have both organizational responsibilities and daily financial responsibilities.

Organizational responsibilities

• Complete the field trip permit (i.e., an authorization form that is approved by the principal; see Form 8-A for an example).

• Meet with the principal to review district procedures for receipting and depositing money collected (e.g., if the group has an after-school meeting and money is collected from the students, do district procedures require a night bank deposit?).

• Research and verify the quality and cost of the vendors who will provide any travel services needed, and if a contract is necessary, forward the information to the principal or designated administrator.

• Identify and locate appropriate receipt forms. If additional receipts are needed, obtain them from the main office. The type of receipt (e.g., individual receipts, a group receipt) depends on district procedures. Form 8-B is a sample individual receipt, and Form 8-C is a sample group receipt.

• Obtain parent/guardian permission for the students to attend the field trip. The permission may include a letter sent to the parents and a form for them to fill out (see Form 8-D for an example).

– Set up a manual or computerized field trip checklist (see Form 8-E) that includes all items and steps needed to have a successful and educational trip (e.g., class roster, a record of parent/guardian permission and contact information, chaperone names, any student medical conditions, notes from an advance visit to the location, designated stops for the trip).

The sponsors are accountable for the field trip (e.g., control of the money collected), so select staff in whom you have a high degree of confidence.

FORM 8-A

Field Trip Authorization and Financial Report
(see Appendix B, p. 130)

FORM 8-B

Individual Receipt (Field Trip)
(see Appendix B, p. 131)

FORM 8-C

Group Receipt (Field Trip)
(see Appendix B, p. 132)

FORM 8-D

Field Trip
Permission Form
(see Appendix B, p. 132)

FORM 8-E

Field Trip Checklist
(see Appendix B, p. 133)

*All field trips must
have principal
approval before
funds are collected
or parental consent
is requested. Trip
sponsors should
complete the financial
report within two
weeks of the trip's
completion, or at the
end of the school year,
whichever comes first.*

Financial responsibilities

- Record money collected from students, using individual receipts or daily group receipt. We recommend issuing individual receipts for dollar amounts above $3. If the amount collected per child is less than $3, a group receipt for the class is fine.

- Compare receipts (individual or group) and money collected, and confirm that the total of all amounts listed on receipts matches the total funds collected (cash and checks).

- Secure the funds collected at the end of the day by forwarding the money to the bookkeeper for deposit or making a night deposit.

➤ **Sponsors' Duties After the Trip**

- Prepare any internal documents required by the school district (e.g., a financial statement; see Form 8-A).

- Verify all vendor charges (e.g., if 40 students went to the museum, the museum charged the correct admission fee for 40 students).

- Discuss the success of the field trip with the principal (e.g., how did it enhance student learning? did the travel service selected provide appropriate student accommodations?).

➤ **Principal's Duties After the Trip**

- Meet with sponsors to review the success of the field trip.

- Make notes on how to improve future field trips (e.g., limit the number of students; use a different bus company).

- Follow district guidelines for refunding any leftover field trip funds. Funds collected for the trip but not spent can be returned to parents by check, or they can remain in the field trip account for that group if the dollar amount per student is low (e.g., $3 or less) and another field trip is planned for the group.

- Review a sample of student work related to the trip (e.g., papers written, posters created) to confirm that the trip was educationally valuable.

Summary

Field trips that are aligned with the district's curriculum are a logical extension of the classroom learning experience. When field trips are being planned, the first step is for an administrator to distribute responsibilities among other staff members. Once responsibilities are clear, proper planning for contracted travel services and daily accounting for the funds collected go a long way toward ensuring that everyone benefits from the trip and all that contractual and financial matters are handled in a businesslike manner. Use the procedures and forms explained in this chapter to assist with your field trips from start to finish.

9

Fund-Raising Events

Fund-Raising Events of Consumable Supplies— *Sales drives sponsored by a school, individual club, or grade level to raise funds for the benefit of the students who participate in the fund-raising activity (e.g., the sale of peanuts by the honor society for a school gift). School groups make a profit by agreeing with a vendor to a predetermined percentage of total sales.*

tip

Use the Internet to look up your school district's purchasing manual and state procurement regulations.

Fund-raising events involving the sale of merchandise ranging from bumper stickers and t-shirts to candy and wrapping paper are a standard part of school life. Increasingly, they are also a valuable source of revenue to cover "extras" that are beyond regular school funding (Vail, 1998).

Unfortunately, when fund-raising events are inadequately planned and poorly organized, your school may be in for a host of financial problems. Reports of lost or missing merchandise and funds may damage the school's image in the community. Staff members may feel obliged to cover losses with personal funds. To avoid these problems, and to enjoy the profits your fund-raising events generate, carefully follow the guidelines in this chapter.

Purchasing Procedures for Fund-Raising Merchandise

Before signing a contract with a merchandise vendor, consider the dollar amount of the contract and what procedures (e.g., formal bid process) you must follow to avoid violating state purchasing laws and district guidelines. Note that violation of the dollar limit set in some state purchasing laws can result in a public employee's dismissal (see *Code of Virginia*, 2002).

- Confirm the appropriate purchasing method for obtaining fund-raising merchandise by answering these three questions:
  - Is a formal bid required?
  - Is a price quote required?
  - Is a purchase order or written contract sufficient?

- Only an authorized school administrator should enter into contracts with merchandise vendors. Prohibit teachers from doing so and have them bring all contracts to you for review, approval, and signature.

Selecting a Merchandise Vendor

Selecting the best merchandise vendor is important to the success of any fund-raising event. Some vendors provide schools with both a good profit percentage (e.g., 50 percent) and an attractive collection of supportive services (e.g., delivery of goods, prepackaging of goods). Always take the time to comparison-shop before signing a contract. Here are some guidelines for evaluating prospective vendors that you will want to discuss with the fund-raising sponsors. (See Figure 9.1 for a graphic summary.)

- Review the vendor's past performance (e.g., does the vendor have a record of offering satisfactory merchandise and service to other schools?).

- Determine the percentage of sales (i.e., the profit) that the vendor is offering the school (e.g., the school will receive 40 percent of gross sales).

- Determine what supportive services the vendor is willing to provide (e.g., prepackaging the sale items for easy distribution to students, setting up the book sale displays, covering the shipping cost for returning unsold items).

- Confirm the vendor's procedure for handling merchandise returned or refused by purchasers (i.e., will the company accept returned or refused items, or is the school required to purchase those items?).

- Review the retail price range of the for-sale items (i.e., are the items within a price range consistent with the students' and parents' purchasing power?).

- Confirm the suitability of the content of the merchandise to be sold (e.g., does the inventory include questionable or controversial materials?).

- Consider the vendor's gift offers. Although it is inappropriate for you to accept personal gifts from a vendor, the school may accept gifts as part of the vendor's contract (e.g., in the case of a book fair, a gift of additional books for the library is appropriate).

tip

Make sure the profit percentage is reasonable for the administrative and student effort required.

FIGURE **9.1**

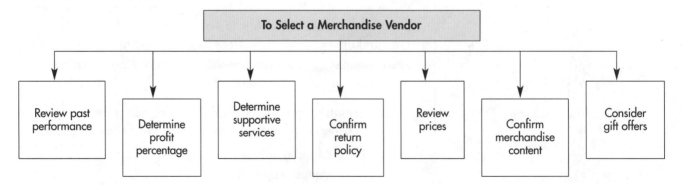

Fund-Raising Responsibilities

Proper planning prior to a fund-raising event helps ensure its overall success and profit. Divide responsibilities among key staff members and make sure that everyone understands your expectations. To guide your organizational efforts, we have outlined the major responsibilities of the principal (or another designated administrator) and the fund-raising event's sponsor before, during, and after the fund-raising event.

➤ Principal's Duties Before the Fund-Raising Event

- Designate the sponsor/teacher who is to handle the event. You may want to coordinate these responsibilities among several staff members. Our guidelines assume one sponsor only.

- Authorize the fund-raising event and meet with the sponsor to review his/her responsibilities before, during, and after the event.

  – Be certain the sponsor understands the duties to be performed every day during the event. It's usually carelessness in the sponsor's daily activities that results in merchandise being misplaced or money being lost or stolen.
  – Confirm that the sponsor understands the district procedure for turning in money collected by staff to the office, to ensure that funds are deposited as required (e.g., if sales occur after school from the students, do district procedures require a night bank deposit?).
  – Be sure that the sponsor is familiar with change fund guidelines and has access to the proper receipt forms.
  – Remind the sponsor that he/she is not at liberty to give away for-sale items to staff or students. Many doughnut sales have ended with the staff having eaten the profits!

- Establish when and to whom items will be sold (e.g., doughnuts will be sold 30 minutes before and after school; 1st graders will visit the book fair at 9:00 a.m. on Monday).

- Establish acceptable payment methods for the sale items (i.e., cash, check, debit and/or credit cards). If debit and credit cards are to be accepted, determine the fee that the school owes to the banks or credit card companies (e.g., the credit card company keeps three percent of the total credit sales).

- Review, approve, and finalize any necessary vendor contracts.

➤ Sponsor's Duties Before the Fund-Raising Event

- Complete a fund-raising permit and submit it to the principal for approval. See Form 9-A for an example.

- Identify and locate appropriate receipt forms. Tracking sales makes it easy to verify the profit percentage your school receives from the vendor. The type of receipt (e.g., a daily sales receipt, individual receipts, cash register tapes) depends on district procedures. Form 9-B is an example of an individual receipt; Form 9-C is an example of a group receipt.

The sponsor is accountable for the fund-raising operations (e.g., control of the inventory and money), so select a person in whom you have a high degree of confidence.

When planning in-school fund-raising sales, always consult school board policies regarding uninterrupted instructional time.

FORM **9-A**

Fund-Raising Event Authorization and Financial Report
(see Appendix B, p. 134)

FORM **9-B**

Individual Receipt
(Fund-Raising)
(see Appendix B, p. 135)

FORM **9-C**

Group Receipt
(Fund-Raising)
(see Appendix B, p. 135)

*All fund-raising
events must have
principal approval
before those events
are announced or
begun.*

FORM **9-D**

Fund-Raising
Event Sponsor's
Distribution List
(see Appendix B, p.136)

• Decide the amount of change fund that will be needed, and submit the change fund request for the principal's approval. There are several important guidelines to follow when using a change fund (University of Virginia, 2002):

– The amount of the change fund remains *constant* for the duration of the fund-raising event.

– A change fund is intended to make small change only, not to make reimbursements, as in a petty cash fund. (See Chapter 13: The Petty Cash Fund for a discussion of the difference in change and petty cash funds.)

– The change fund should be kept in a locked box with compartments for coins and bills; the box should be stored in a locked area with limited access.

– As a rule of thumb, a change fund should be deposited into the school's checking account at the end of the fund-raising event.

• For fund-raising events like book fairs or holiday bazaars, set a duty roster and schedule for volunteer staff and parents to ensure adequate staffing throughout all hours of operation. The schedule provides an easy reference tool should problems like sales or receipting errors arise.

• Verify the quality and quantity of inventory received.

• Secure the inventory to prevent loss or damage (e.g., the storage area can be locked; key access is limited).

► Sponsor's Duties During the Fund-Raising Event

Sponsors should perform a number of duties daily throughout the course of the fund-raising event.

• Organize the participants selling items for adequate record keeping. If items such as tins of peanuts are to be distributed to students to sell, make an accurate distribution list of who received the items and the number of items each student received. See Form 9-D for an example.

• Record daily sales with individual receipts (see Form 9-B) or a daily group sales receipt (see Form 9-C).

• Reconcile daily receipts and money collected (e.g., compare the total of the amount listed on the receipts to the total amount of funds collected).

• Secure the funds collected at the end of the day and adhere to district guidelines for turning in money collected by staff (e.g., forward the money to the bookkeeper for deposit; make a night deposit, if necessary). Store the change fund in a locked box in a secure location.

• Secure the inventory (e.g., lock the inventory in a room; limit key access).

See Figure 9.2 for a graphic summary of these points.

FIGURE **9.2**

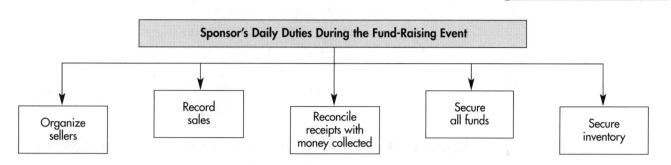

➤ Sponsor's Duties After the Fund-Raising Event

• Count ending inventory (all unsold merchandise) before returning it to the vendor.

• Prepare any internal documents required by the school district as soon as possible, before the details pertaining to the fund raiser are forgotten. Form 9-A includes a sample financial report. Make a notation of any items still owed by students or staff, such as money or merchandise (e.g., unsold tins of peanuts).

• Verify that the school received the appropriate percentage of total sales based on the agreement between the school and the vendor (e.g., if the school is to receive 40 percent of the sales, multiple the total gross sales by .4). The percentage of the total sales is the school's profit, assuming that all expenses are paid.

• Return the change fund to the bookkeeper for deposit in the school's checking account.

• Discuss the success of the event with administrative staff (e.g., was it profitable? was it beneficial to students and parents?).

See Figure 9.3 for a graphic summary of these points.

tip

The event sponsor should complete the financial report within two weeks of the event's ending date, or at the end of the school year, whichever comes first.

FIGURE **9.3**

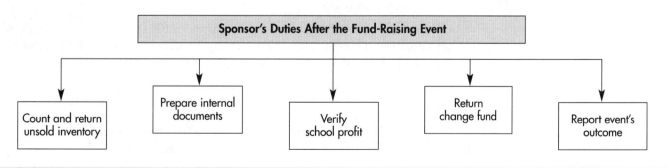

➤ **Principal's Duties After the Fund-Raising Event**

- Review the success of the fund-raising event with the sponsor.
- Make notes concerning ways to improve future events (e.g., limit the amount of inventory students receive to reduce the amount of loss from errors in record keeping or theft).
- Finalize plans to spend the money on the school group that raised the funds as specified in the fund-raising permit.

Special Safeguards for "Big Fund-Raising Events"

Some fund-raising events, such as school picture sales or the sale of class rings, are held annually or semiannually and involve major potential revenue for the school. Central office purchasing staff often negotiate the district contract so that one vendor serves all schools. Frequently, the orders and funds received, although collected by the school, are never processed through the school's bookkeeping system; instead, the vendor's representatives periodically pick up receipts from the school office throughout the course of the fund-raising event. Once the event is over, the vendor forwards a check to the school based on the percentage of total sales outlined in the district contract.

This system is convenient for the school, but also fraught with potential opportunities for loss or theft. Essentially, there are no verification controls in place to prevent loss or theft by the teacher collecting funds, the office staff receiving funds, or the vendor. Here are some safeguards to help you protect the funds that "pass through" your office and, thus, protect your school's potential profit.

- Insist that teachers turn in all money collected every day.
- Require a vendor's representative to pick up receipts every day.
- Lock up funds that are in the office, waiting for vendor pick-up.
- Arrange for a school staff member *and* a vendor's representative to jointly count the funds collected each day.
- Insist that the vendor give the school a receipt for funds collected each day.
- Retain all receipts and tally them at the end of the event. This figure is the total sales for your school.
- Compare the profit check from the vendor with (1) the total of your written receipts from the vendor and (2) the contracted percentage of the total sales (e.g., 40 percent of a total sales of $10,000 equals $4,000).

Summary

Fund-raising events can provide a valuable service to the school community in the form of much needed revenue and desirable merchandise. Additionally, these events can teach students important lessons about economics, if the events are discussed and carried out with instruction in mind. However, the opportunity for loss of funds and merchandise is high if fund-raising events are poorly organized and insufficiently monitored. The guidelines in this chapter, if followed, will prevent major problems so that your school community can enjoy fund-raising events and benefit from the profits these events generate.

10

Gifts to Students or Staff

Gifts to Students or Staff—*Personal goods or services for students or staff purchased with school funds. Gifts for staff members include items purchased for personal use (e.g., baby shower items) and exclude items purchased by the school or the district for the staff's use at school (e.g., bulletin board supplies, hand calculators, school desk accessories). A rule of thumb for determining if an item is a gift is to ask, "Does the item leave the school when the teacher transfers or terminates?"*

Educators are generally very thoughtful, and giving gifts to celebrate special events or achievements is a natural part of school life. Just like all other transactions involving the expenditure of funds, however, gift giving at your school should be governed by a set of guidelines. Always remember that school funds are not yours to loan, borrow, or give away. This pertains to using funds to purchase gifts, too—even when the reasons for the gifts are good. Follow the simple guidelines in this chapter to avoid the appearance of poor judgment or impropriety in the occasional giving of gifts in your school.

Gifts to Students

Gifts or prizes for students paid for from school activity funds are appropriate only (1) as "incentives" for fund-raising events and, (2) as awards for special achievement. Here is an overview of what you need to know about giving gifts to students. (See Figure 10.1 for a graphic summary.)

➤ **Fund-Raising Incentive Gifts**

- If gifts are part of a fund-raising incentive, they should be given only to students who participated in the fund-raising event. Make sure that a prize is age appropriate and does not affect the overall profitability of the event (e.g., expensive bicycles).

- Incentive gifts for students should be purchased with funds raised by the particular student group that will receive the gifts. For example, do not use money in the student government

When giving gifts, remember to keep public opinion in mind. You do not want to give the impression that school money is being spent recklessly.

account to pay for gifts that reward students for work on behalf of the future business leaders club.

- Gifts that are not related to fund raising should not favor one group of students over another (e.g., birthday pencils only for Mrs. Jones's class).

➤ Special Achievement Gifts

Schools typically hold academic awards assemblies and athletic banquets at least once a year. At these school events, individual students and teams are recognized for special achievements, and awards are often given to commemorate the occasion.

- Gifts and awards should be nominal in value and age appropriate.
- Funding for awards may come from the general fund, donations from businesses or parent groups, or (in the case of sports awards) from the athletic fund.

FIGURE 10.1

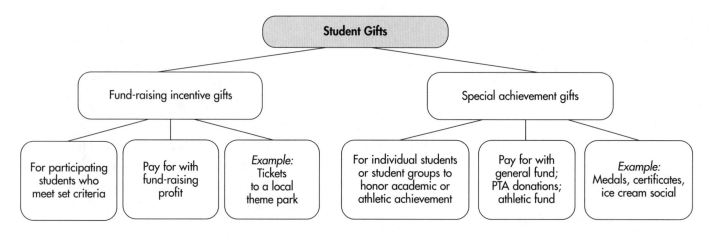

Gifts to Staff Members

The giving of gifts to staff members should be guided by written procedures and coordinated by a committee, not an individual staff member. The group should meet at least once a year to review guidelines and the contribution amount to the staff remembrance fund (which should be the major source of staff gifts). Here is an overview of what you need to know about giving gifts to staff. (See Figure 10.2 for a graphic summary.)

➤ Special Occasion Gifts
- When school procedures allow gifts to staff members, the gifts should be reasonably priced and (usually) paid for with staff remembrance funds. Most schools establish a remembrance fund to acknowledge staff members' life events (e.g., a wedding or a new baby, a death in the family).

– The money in a staff remembrance fund comes from annual dues and staff donations (*never* from student funds) or is raised specifically by the staff (e.g., profits from the drink machine in the staff lounge).

– The staff remembrance fund should be managed by a committee in accordance with a set of written procedures, including dollar limits for staff gifts and the types of appropriate gifts. Rotate committee membership every year.

– The staff remembrance committee should meet at least once a year to review guidelines for using and contributing to the staff remembrance fund.

➤ Fund-Raising Incentive Gifts

• If staff members participate in a fund-raising project (e.g., school t-shirt sale), then a gift to a staff member may be appropriate (e.g., a gift to the highest seller).

• Because gift expenses should be subtracted from the generated profit, keep the gift items reasonable in cost and no more than 5 percent of the overall profit.

➤ All-Staff Gifts

• Token gifts given at the opening of the school year or during teacher appreciation week should be nominal in cost and, generally, paid for with staff-generated funds set aside or donated (e.g., by the PTA) for this purpose.

– As a rule of thumb, if the staff generates the funds, it is appropriate to use the funds to benefit the staff. Profits from the teacher's lounge drink machine or from doughnut or bake sales held among the staff may be used for teacher incentive items. Raffles held among the staff for premium parking places are another popular way to raise funds for staff gifts.

– When an all-school fund-raising event, such as school pictures sales, is held and teachers purchase pictures, the percentage of the profit raised by the staff may be spent on the staff.

– Some school districts allow money for incentive or recognition gifts to staff to come from the general fund, as long as the gifts are inexpensive (e.g., no more than $5 per person) and useful in the classroom. We recommend limiting this practice. Because the general fund comes primarily from the profits of projects involving the entire student body (e.g., school picture sales), this money should be spent in ways that benefit the entire school community—not just the staff. If in doubt about this practice, refer to your district's guidelines regarding appropriate expenditures from your general fund.

• Cash or cash equivalent items (e.g., checks, gift certificates that are redeemable for cash) should not be given to staff members unless the amount is added the employee's Form W-2 for income tax purposes. The Internal Revenue Service (2003b) considers gifts of cash as extra earnings that are subject to taxation. We recommend that all staff gifts be tangible items of low dollar value so that they cannot be construed as disguised wages.

FIGURE **10.2**

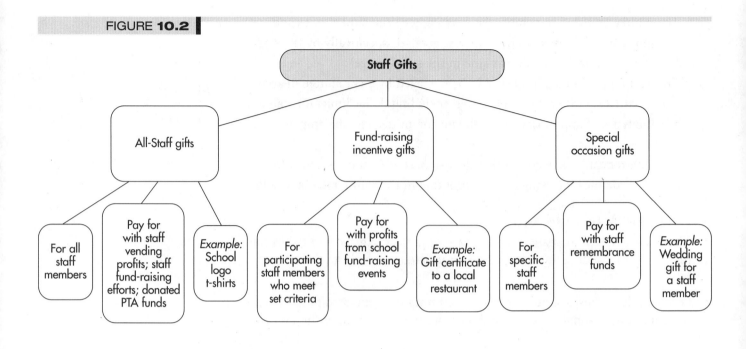

Special Efforts for Specific Students or Staff Members

On rare occasions, schools undertake special collections or fund-raising projects to benefit a staff member or student who is coping with illness or a catastrophic event. It's a good idea to seek advice from your district accounting department before approving a fund-raising event earmarked for this purpose. Remember that any cash or cash equivalent a school employee receives from the school—even when received in special circumstances—is part of that employee's taxable wages and must be reported to the district payroll office. Overall, the best approach is to ask a parent organization within your school community (e.g., the PTA) to coordinate any benefit event or campaign on the school's behalf, with a local bank handling the collected funds. Generally, it is unwise to have these funds accounted in your bookkeeping records and by your bookkeeping staff.

Summary

Thoughtful acts are a natural part of the social interaction in schools. However, when gifts and prizes are purchased with funds accounted for by the school, procedural guidelines are necessary to ensure proper accountability. It is very important to avoid the appearance of poor judgment within your school and community in the giving of gifts or prizes, even when these items are given with the best of intentions. By implementing the suggestions in this chapter, you can prevent an act of kindness from turning into an administrative headache.

11

Online Purchasing and Electronic Banking Transfers

Online Purchasing—*Using the Internet to order goods or services for school use. Safeguards are necessary to ensure financial security comparable with paper purchase orders and "snail mail" processing. Technically, online purchasing is a type of electronic fund transfer that authorizes payment for a product or service over the Internet.*

Electronic Banking Transfer—*A monetary transaction initiated through an electronic terminal, telephone, or computer to authorize a financial institution to add or deduct funds from an account. Electronic banking transfers allow you to move money from one account to another without writing a traditional check to authorize the transaction.*

In this age of computers, many schools are increasing efficiency by incorporating electronic services available via the Internet into their bookkeeping functions. These computer transactions allow your bookkeeper to process vendor orders or transfer money between school bank accounts from an office computer, thereby saving time and paperwork. We discuss online purchasing and electronic banking transfers together in this chapter because both processes require similar safeguards, both make use of the Internet, and both are technically the electronic transfer of funds.

Basic Information

Online purchasing allows for faster ordering and, in many instances, a vendor will discount your order because of reduced processing expenses to fill the order. Remember, in these transactions, it's your staff—not the vendor's—that is entering the order. Once the order is received, the vendor sends an order confirmation, often by e-mail, for your approval. The actual amount of the order is drafted from your school bank account or credit/purchasing card each month, with any discrepancies adjusted on the next billing statement. Some vendors issue their invoices by account code, which helps your bookkeeper quickly match the bill amount to the correct account code in your school's records.

In the same way, electronic banking transfers allow your school to process a payment for goods or services by means of online payments. They also allow you to electronically transfer funds from one school account to another (e.g., transfers from checking

The principal's "signature" is still required in electronic purchases.

Research reliable vendors before ordering online.

to savings). In either case, care should be taken to ensure that money is recorded in the school's bookkeeping system promptly so that these transactions can be tracked when bank statements arrive. It is also very important that security measures be followed to ensure that all transactions are *authorized.* The remainder of this chapter is designed to give you, the principal, important information about the safeguards necessary when establishing either an online purchasing or an electronic banking transfer process at your school.

Controls for Online Purchasing and Electronic Banking Transfers

As with any financial process, the best place to prevent error or theft is at the initial point of the transaction. For both online purchasing and electronic banking transfers, minimize your exposure to error and loss by asking the vendor (in online purchasing) or the bank (in electronic transfer of funds) for limitations. In this section, we have listed guidelines for reducing the risk associated with using these transaction procedures. Graphic overviews of our recommendations are presented in Figure 11.1 (online purchasing procedures) and Figure 11.2 (electronic bank transfer procedures).

➤ Online Purchasing

• Check with other schools or school districts to find those that have used a vendor's online processing system and can report good results. Ask for the names of effective online vendors and for specific examples of increased efficiency resulting from online purchasing.

• Do not buy from any vendor who does not have a written purchasing agreement on file with your school district. Select online vendors from a slate that has been "pre-approved" by the district; written vendor agreements are normally negotiated by a central office purchasing department.

• Direct your staff to buy from only a few of the district-approved vendors. By restricting online purchasing to a limited number of vendors, you help to ensure staff familiarity with online purchasing processes. This safeguard is particularly important in the initial stages of online purchasing implementation.

• Require each vendor to provide documentation that its Web site has the secure firewalls necessary to protect your bank account number from online thieves.

• Require approval for all online orders. It is a good idea to limit the approval of online orders to you and your school computer. Your district's written vendor agreements should include procedures specifying that vendors will accept only those orders bearing your electronic signature and transmitted from your computer. Once your bookkeeper has processed an order electronically, he/she should transmit it to your computer for your "electronic signature." At that point, it is transmitted to the company. This internal transfer capability is a desirable feature to request in the vendor agreement, as it reduces the risk of unauthorized purchases. Limit access and passwords necessary for placing orders to yourself, your bookkeeper, and one administrative staff member (e.g., an assistant principal).

- Make sure that your district's information technology department has reviewed your school's system security (e.g., you have the latest virus protection, your system has installed hacker-protection software).

FIGURE **11.1**

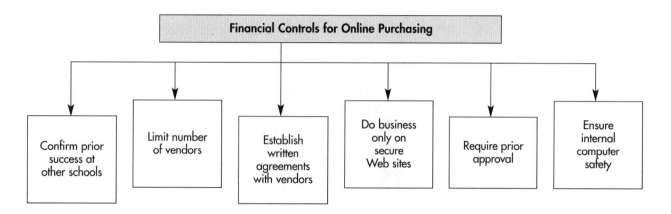

```
                Financial Controls for Online Purchasing
```

| Confirm prior success at other schools | Limit number of vendors | Establish written agreements with vendors | Do business only on secure Web sites | Require prior approval | Ensure internal computer safety |

➤ Electronic Banking Transfers

- Discuss other schools' experience with electronic banking transfers before you begin. As with online purchasing, it's best to benefit from the experience of others. Ask specifically about the clarity of the monthly bank statement and the ease of correcting errors.

- Exercise care when establishing controls over electronic transfer of funds. It is critical that your information technology department ensure a secure line (i.e., one where no one can intercept the transaction). If your computer group cannot confirm a secure connection, reconsider transferring funds electronically.

- Obtain a written agreement with the bank and submit it to your school board attorney and your district's accounting department for independent review and approval. Better yet, ask your accounting/purchasing departments to negotiate an arrangement with a bank.

- Require the transaction to be posted in your bookkeeping system *before* it is entered at the bank to ensure that this step is not overlooked on a busy day.

- Restrict where funds may be transferred to and from (e.g., funds from the school's checking account may only be transferred to the school's savings account and the joint investment account for the school district).

- Require principal approval for all transfers. It is a good idea to limit the approval and confirmation of electronic fund transfers to you at your school e-mail address. Make sure that this limitation is a part of the written agreement with the bank.

- Decide if you are going to allow only computer transfers or transfers by both computer and telephone. The addition of phone transactions may increase risk, as the accessibility can make it easier to circumvent the approval process.

tip

Learn from the experience and expertise of others before initiating electronic banking transfers.

- Understand your liability and your rights as a consumer if an unauthorized banking transfer occurs (Federal Deposit Insurance Corporation, 1993):

  – As a consumer, you must report any unauthorized transfers of funds within 60 days of receiving your monthly statement from the bank. Failure to do so makes your school liable for transactions that occurred after the 60 days and before the date that you notified the bank of the error.

  – You may be required to follow up in writing within 10 days if you notified the bank by phone or in person.

  – In turn, the institution is required to investigate the error within 10 business days of your notification and inform you of findings within 3 days of the investigation's conclusion. If the institution cannot complete its investigation within the 10-day period, your school may be eligible for a temporary account credit in the amount of the alleged error (including interest, if applicable) until the bank's investigation is complete.

FIGURE **11.2**

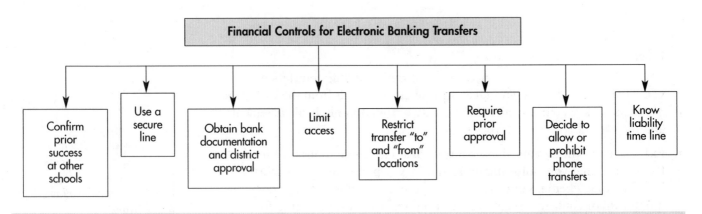

Financial Controls for Electronic Banking Transfers

Confirm prior success at other schools | Use a secure line | Obtain bank documentation and district approval | Limit access | Restrict transfer "to" and "from" locations | Require prior approval | Decide to allow or prohibit phone transfers | Know liability time line

Written Procedures for Online Purchasing and Electronic Banking Transfers

Written procedures should include enough information to assist individuals making and approving the transactions, but not so much information that they allow an unauthorized user to gain access (Chesney, 1999). For example, you should never include passwords or login names in your procedures manual. Here are some other safeguards that you want to address in your written procedures.

- Address separation of duties and explicitly state that the person who places an order or a banking transfer cannot approve that transaction.

- Include an employee agreement that contains specific legal language advising users that misuse (e.g., ordering personal items) is punishable by severe penalties, including possible termination of employment. Because purchasing, accounting, and personnel guidelines differ from district to district, it is advisable to have your school board attorney approve employee agreements prior to their use.

- Require training before a user is authorized to perform transactions. Staff should not have access rights until they have completed at least one training seminar on proper procedures and appropriate safeguards.

- Specify allowable dollar limits for both purchases and electronic banking transfers.

- Require audits that test the security of your computer system and other controls (e.g., limitations on where money can be transferred and dollar limits).

- Require passwords to be changed on a periodic basis (e.g., every 30, 60, or 90 days).

- Include procedures outlining what to do when the designated authorizing staff members are unavailable to approve transactions. This may require a delay in processing or the use of traditional purchasing and banking methods. State explicitly that under no circumstances should staff share passwords.

- Address any additional steps needed for confirming the reconciliation of the school's bank statement (e.g., approval by you within 10 days after the statement arrives), as electronic banking transfers do appear on bank statements by date or in a separate section.

Summary

Online purchasing and electronic funds transfers reduce a school's paperwork. When you purchase items online, the reduced processing time can allow vendors to offer larger discounts. Items ordered often arrive faster, because vendors don't have to wait for a paper purchase order to be delivered through traditional mail. Essentially, online purchasing and electronic banking transfers are similar to what you might do at home when you order airline tickets via the Internet, arrange to have the power company automatically deduct your monthly electric bill from your checking account, or take advantage of your bank's online banking services to move funds between accounts.

The biggest differences between these kinds of electronic transactions at home and school are the additional controls necessary: the written agreements with banks and vendors and the formal approval process. The wise principal ensures that the proper safeguards are in place to prevent theft and unauthorized "borrowing" of the school's purchasing power. Follow the guidelines in this chapter and enjoy the benefits of the computer age.

12

Parent Organizations

Parent Organizations—
Private, parent-run organizations that support school projects through the donation of money, equipment, and services. All parent organization funds are accounted for and reported separately from school activity funds, in accordance with the regulations of the Internal Revenue Service (IRS).

Active parent organizations, such the National Congress of Parents and Teachers Association (PTA), athletic booster clubs, and booster clubs for band and chorus, play an important role in the school community and add to a school's health and vitality. These groups often engage in major fund-raising activities and, in turn, donate much needed money, materials, equipment, and services that limited district budgets sometimes cannot provide.

The school principal's role in the financial matters of parent organizations is advisory only. Because parent groups are independent entities, the funds they raise are private and the principal is not fiscally responsible for their management. However, parent organizations will look to you, the principal, for leadership on many subjects, including financial matters. A knowledgeable principal can provide appropriate guidance to parent groups and help prevent the money problems that sometimes arise and cause embarrassment for the school community.

Routine Responsibilities of a Parent Organization Treasurer

According to the National PTA (2000), treasurers in parent organizations typically perform the following duties:

– Maintain accurate, detailed records in a permanent system, whether manual or electronic.
– Receipt collected funds.
– Deposit funds in an authorized bank account with an IRS Employer Identification Number.

– Pay all approved bills by check, requiring two signatures.

– Balance the monthly bank statement.

– Reconcile the organization's books with the monthly bank statement.

– Prepare written financial reports for group meetings.

– Answer financial questions clearly and directly.

– Prepare financial records for audit.

– Assist with the transfer of financial records from the past three to five years to a new treasurer before stepping down from the treasurer position.

Periodically, meet informally with presidents of parent organizations to discuss financial matters within their groups. Be alert to any warning signs that organization treasurers are not performing routine financial functions well.

Budget Preparation in Parent Organizations

A well-functioning parent organization goes through an annual budget process, with a budget committee preparing an estimated, one-year budget on behalf of the group. Parent organization budgets should be available for public review and should contain the follow elements:

– Projected income and expenditures based on at least a three-year history.

– Projected expenditures balanced by equal sources of income.

– Sufficient detail to clarify proposed projects and the means of paying for them.

– Formal approval by the organization in an open meeting of the membership, with approval documented in written minutes.

– Procedures to amend the budget, as needed, with approval of the organization.

As a rule, ask each parent organization president to provide a copy of the group's budget at the start of the school year. Offer suggestions on the budget process as needed, but maintain your advisory role.

Fund-Raising Procedures for Parent Organizations

Raising money to carry out budgeted projects consumes much of a parent organization's time and energy. Each organization's president is responsible for seeing that the organization follows standard accounting practices with regard to these funds. Here is an overview of the necessary procedures. (See Figure 12.1 for a graphic summary.)

• Organizations should issue prenumbered receipts for goods and services sold and for all membership fees.

• The treasurer and a second organization member should count the cash received and reconcile that amount to the receipts given. Both should sign a document specifying the total amount to be deposited.

Treasurers should never keep organization funds in their homes or deposit this money into personal accounts.

Make sure the treasurers of parent organizations are bonded.

Remember that even a well-prepared budget is at best only an estimate of income and expenditures. Periodic adjustments are a normal part of the budget process.

- The treasurer should stamp all checks received with "For Deposit Only" and the organization's bank account number.

- Funds raised should be deposited promptly in the organization's bank account. The treasurer should make night deposits if necessary and always retain copies of deposit records.

- The organization treasurer should prepare a written financial statement summarizing the expenses and profit from the fund-raising event and submit it to the group's president within five days.

- The organization treasurer should prepare a written report for the group on the financial outcome of the fund-raising event and submit it for discussion during the first group meeting following the event.

FIGURE **12.1**

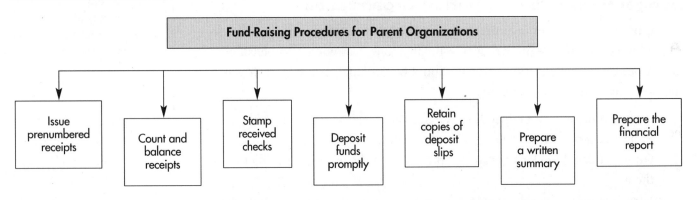

A principal's insight into the financial workings of parent organizations often varies from group to group. For example, because you serve as member of the PTA's executive board, that group's reliance on fund-raising safeguards should be very evident to you, whereas with groups such as the band boosters, you may need to inquire into procedures. If a parent organization's fund-raising safeguards are not clearly evident, do not hesitate to open a conversation about money matters and offer general guidance to that group's leadership team.

School Staff Involvement with Parent Organization Fund Raising

Generally, school staff should avoid collecting funds on behalf of a parent organization (or any other private group). Designated organization members should bear total responsibility for the collection and receipting of funds.

If you decide to make an exception to this rule, (e.g., PTA dues or United Way donations collected by classroom teachers at the start of the school year), we recommend you take precautions to prevent these funds from inadvertently mixing with "school money." Prepare a written agreement ahead of time to be signed by you and the head of the parent organization. This agreement should clarify the following points.

- Require organizations to provide unique donation envelopes. To help ensure that the envelopes are not opened before they reach the organization's treasurer, parents and other contributors should be directed to seal their envelope and to sign across the seal.

- Require organizations to issue return receipts acknowledging these contributions.

- Consider additional security controls, such as providing a mounted, locked box in the office area, temporarily designated for the organization to hold collected funds and requesting that organization representatives collect funds daily.

- Require each organization to account for collected funds in a bookkeeping system designated for its exclusive use. Private money must never be deposited in school activity accounts, for which the school bears full legal responsibility.

Audits of Parent Organizations

Audits of parent organizations serve the same purpose as the audits of a school's bookkeeping records: to verify that these records accurately represent financial activity during the audit period and that appropriate financial procedures are being followed.

- An outside audit of the organization's financial records assures the membership that funds are being collected and expended as reported by the treasurer and that records are kept according to standard accounting practices. An auditor selects a representative sample of financial transactions and follows the transactions as recorded in the treasurer's records (e.g., checkbook, bank statements, ledger). At the conclusion of the sampling process, the auditor determines if the samples indicate that the current financial records are accurate for the period of time specified.

- Most organizations use an audit committee composed of members who may or may not be familiar with audit procedures. If the audit committee has any concerns regarding the findings, an independent audit by an accountant who is either a certified public accountant (CPA) or a certified internal auditor (CIA) is recommended.

- The principal should expect parent organizations to be independently audited under two routine conditions: (1) annually, at the close of the school year; (2) when a treasurer resigns and before a new treasurer begins.

Financial Warning Signs

You may wish to speak with a parent organization's leader if any of the following conditions are evident:

– Organization funds are kept in private homes.
– Authorized check signers are in the same family.
– Blank checks are signed.
– Checks are made payable to "Cash."

– Unauthorized purchases are made.
– The school bookkeeper serves as the organization's treasurer.
– Receipts are not issued for collected funds.
– One person counts all received funds.
– Bank statements are not balanced monthly.
– One person receives, records, and deposits funds.
– Board meetings, treasurer's reports, and minutes are rare.

The Principal's Role if Theft is Suspected

• If you become aware that theft may have occurred at the hands of a member of a parent organization, immediately contact your district accounting office. (If your school district is a large one, chances are that this will not be the first case of suspected theft within the district.) The district office can offer advice on how to proceed.

• Lend a sympathetic ear to those within the organization who have discovered the theft, but maintain your advisory role and allow the organization to solve the problem. It may be helpful to suggest the following course of action to the group's leadership:

– The highest-ranking officer in the organization should immediately obtain and secure bookkeeping records, such as checkbooks, bank statements, and ledgers.
– An officer should contact the district-wide group (e.g., regional PTA), if one exists, to obtain advice and support.
– Conversations with individuals under suspicion should be documented as to time, place, and comments.
– Reputable audit services should be obtained at once to review bookkeeping records.

General Advice About Nonprofit Groups

• It is important that you allow only tax-exempt organizations, as specified by the Internal Revenue Code (Internal Revenue Service, 2000), to function within the school community as nonprofit groups. For example, a community group may want to offer student programs (e.g., athletic camps) as a nonprofit organization, yet may not have nonprofit status with the IRS. A qualified organization will have proof of its IRS review and a tax-exempt identification number, which signifies that it has met two tests (National PTA Annual Resources, 2000):

– *Organizational Test.* The IRS tests the purpose of an organization by examining documents like bylaws and articles of incorporation.
– *Operational Test.* The IRS tests the operations of an organization by reviewing its activities, source of funds, and distribution of funds.

• Accept donations of equipment only as allowed by district policies (e.g., only compatible computers). Otherwise, you may be obligating your school for installation and long-term maintenance costs.

- Encourage groups to incur financial obligations on behalf of the school only when clear financial support is available within the current school year. Discourage expensive, long-term projects, because such projects may obligate future patrons without their express consent.

- Allow only properly insured parent organizations to sponsor or undertake day care programs, athletic camps, or any other project where insurance is prudent.

As questions arise, seek the advice of your district's financial officers; they will be glad to help with the answers.

Summary

Parent organizations provide a tremendous service in support of the school community. In terms of the organization's finances, the principal's role is strictly advisory. The wise principal, however, understands the principles of basic money management and is in a position to give prudent advice to the group's leadership if warning signs of financial mismanagement emerge. Like all groups, parent organizations can do much to avoid financial problems by diligently following the basic rules for handling funds.

13

The Petty Cash Fund

Petty Cash Fund—
A limited fund of bills and coins (e.g., $50–100) used for the reimbursement of small, unexpected school-related purchases where it is impractical to issue frequent, individual checks.

The establishment and use of a petty cash fund offers a convenient way to cover unexpected expenses related to school events such as dances, pageants, and plays. With a small amount of cash available in the school, staff members can receive quick reimbursement for inexpensive last-minute or emergency purchases without going through the purchase order procedure or using the school credit card.

There are two possible approaches to school petty cash: (1) staff members spend personal money on school business and then receive reimbursement from the school's petty cash fund; or (2) staff members receive money from the petty cash fund, spend it on school business, and then reconcile, or "settle up," the difference between the advanced amount and the actual cost to staff, as documented in the original receipt.

We highly recommend the first approach—using the petty cash fund to reimburse authorized expenditures of personal funds—and this approach is the basis for the recommendations in this chapter. Requiring staff to spend personal money first enables a school to verify the exact amount needed for reimbursement. Under the model we recommend, after a staff member receives a cash reimbursement for an approved expense (e.g., purchasing the extra extension cord needed to plug in the light board for a school play), the bookkeeper replaces the amount of cash paid out when the fund is reconciled by transferring funds from the appropriate activity fund account (e.g., the drama club account) to the petty cash fund. In contrast, a school that allows staff to request petty cash before making a purchase is placing an unnecessary burden on the bookkeeper, who must process the paperwork (including obtaining the principal's signature), hand out the cash, and adjust the paperwork if staff find that they need more or less petty cash than anticipated.

Always remember that cash maintained on site is particularly vulnerable to misuse or theft, and school staff must carefully follow specific procedures to ensure its security. Fortunately, these procedures are not difficult to establish. This chapter explains what you need to know about setting up and maintaining a secure petty cash fund so that you and your staff can enjoy the benefits it provides and minimize the associated drawbacks (see Figure 13.1).

FIGURE **13.1**

Benefits and Drawbacks of a Petty Cash Fund

Benefits	Drawbacks
Reduces the number of checks written to purchase inexpensive items.	Always cash in the building overnight.
Allows staff to receive rapid reimbursement for small, out-of-pocket expenses.	Potential for "conflict" if staff members ask to borrow money or use the fund to cash personal checks.
Allows for fast and easy purchasing of emergency items.	Potential for theft and misuse, unless strict accounting procedures are followed.

Establishing a Petty Cash Fund

This section assumes that there is currently no petty cash fund in your school and you wish to start one. (If a petty cash fund already exists at your school, it may be wise to check your district's rules regarding these funds to make sure that you have current approval.)

- Seek and secure written permission from the appropriate district financial officer. The approval request should include the requested dollar amount of the petty cash fund, the name of the person who will be responsible for the fund, the reason the fund is needed, and the measures your school will take to secure the fund (e.g., the fund will be kept in a fireproof, locked cabinet).

- Appoint a "custodian" of the petty cash fund (i.e., the person responsible for disbursing actual cash, probably your bookkeeper).

- Once you receive permission to establish the petty cash fund, issue a check from your activity fund checking account to "Petty Cash" in the approved amount. The custodian of the fund is responsible for cashing the check at the school's bank.

- Place the petty cash in a secure location with limited key access.

Written Procedures for Using a Petty Cash Fund

Keep written procedures regarding the operation of your petty cash fund on file in your school and include them in your staff handbook. It's important that

Make sure the staff member responsible for the fund is covered under the school district's fidelity bond.

copies of the procedures be available at the beginning of each school year so that all staff members understand the procedures ahead of time—before they spend their own money and before they come to the office looking to "borrow" petty cash to buy lunch or to cash a check. Here are some points to cover in your written petty cash fund procedures.

- Establish the dollar limit of petty cash payments (e.g., no payments over $25).
- Determine the type of payments to be processed (e.g., small, nonrecurring purchases, but no travel expenses, gifts, or flowers).
- Prohibit staff from using this fund to cash personal checks or obtain a personal loan. The petty cash fund is for *school business only*.
- Establish a regular schedule for reconciling (balancing and replenishing) the petty cash fund (e.g., once a week, once a month).
- Clarify which staff positions are eligible to be reimbursed from the fund (e.g., athletic director, drama club sponsor).
- Determine who may approve expenditures from petty cash (e.g., an assistant principal and the principal).
- Clarify what will happen when the fund custodian is unavailable to process petty cash disbursements (e.g., no payments will be made; a co-custodian is responsible).
- Establish security for petty cash (e.g., only the fund custodian and the principal have access to the lock box key).
- Require the use of prenumbered petty cash vouchers (see Form 13-A for a completed example) and the submission of supporting documentation (e.g., a store receipt).
- Encourage staff to anticipate purchases and arrange for payment by purchase order or school credit/purchasing card whenever possible. Stress that this fund is for event "emergencies."

Making Payments from the Petty Cash Fund

- Process all disbursements from the petty cash with a petty cash reimbursement voucher (see Form 13-A).
- Attach supporting documentation (e.g., vendor's invoice, cash register receipt) to the voucher. Accept only original store documents for approved school expenses.
- Keep the voucher and supporting documentation in the petty cash box until reimbursement is received from the appropriate activity fund account.
- Make sure an authorized administrator approves the voucher before payment. The approval process follows the same guidelines as other payments from activity funds made by check, with the principal reviewing and approving documentation prior to payment.
- The person receiving the cash payment (the payee) signs the voucher, indicating that money for reimbursement has been received.

See Figure 13.2 for a graphic summary of these guidelines.

tip

Petty cash guidelines should include the obvious (e.g., petty cash payments cannot be mailed; no loans are allowed).

FORM 13-A

Petty Cash
Reimbursement
Voucher
(see Appendix B, p. 137)

FIGURE **13.2**

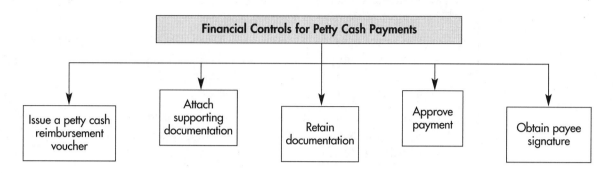

Reconciling the Petty Cash Fund

A petty cash fund should be balanced or "reconciled" on a regular basis (weekly, if the fund is used actively; monthly if it is not used actively). You, as the principal, should check to see that the fund custodian (typically, the school bookkeeper) prepares reconciliations as scheduled in your school's written petty cash fund procedures. See Form 13-B for an example of a petty cash reconciliation form.

FORM **13-B**

Petty Cash
Reconciliation
Form
(see Appendix B, p. 137)

- The purpose of reconciling the petty cash fund is to make sure that no money is missing (i.e., the original amount of the fund is accounted for by a combination of cash and completed vouchers) and to maintain the authorized amount of petty cash by replacing funds used to reimburse staff expenses with funds from the appropriate activity accounts.

- As illustrated in Form 13-B, the total expenditures on the reconciliation form (e.g., $35) is the amount needed to reimburse the petty cash fund. The bookkeeper writes a check in this amount (payable to "Petty Cash") for the principal's signature and records the expenditures in the appropriate activity fund accounts (e.g., the honor society account, the general fund, the drama club account). In the Form 13-B example, the bookkeeper records a $15 decrease in the general fund account for postage and a $20 decrease in the fund account for small maintenance expenditures.

- Once a month, have someone other than the fund custodian (e.g., an assistant principal) count the petty cash in the presence of the fund custodian (Virginia Commonwealth University, 2002).

- The money on hand plus the vouchers for reimbursement should equal the total amount of the petty cash fund. For example, if the petty cash fund amount is $250, the cash on hand plus the reimbursement vouchers equals $250 at all times. Once a check to reimburse the fund is written and cashed, the cash amount of the fund is again $250.

The Petty Cash Fund vs. a Change Fund

It is important not to confuse a petty cash fund with a change fund. Here is some clarification on the similarities and differences (University of Virginia, 2002). See Figure 13.3 for a graphic representation.

- Unlike a petty cash fund, a change fund is *not* used for reimbursement. It is intended to make small change when patrons are buying items such as bumper stickers or admission tickets.

- The actual amount of money in a petty cash box varies when reimbursements to the fund are pending. The actual amount in a change fund drawer remains constant for the duration of the fund (e.g., $10 for an elementary school store, $50 for a secondary school store).

- A school has only one petty cash fund. It can have several activity-specific change funds open at the same time (e.g., a school store change fund, a bake sale change fund).

- A petty cash fund continues throughout the school year. As a rule of thumb, a change fund is deposited into the school's checking account at the end a specific event (e.g., basketball game).

- Loans and the cashing of personal checks are not allowed for either fund.

- Both petty cash funds and change funds should be stored in a locked area with limited key access.

FIGURE 13.3

Features of a
Petty Cash Fund
and Change Fund

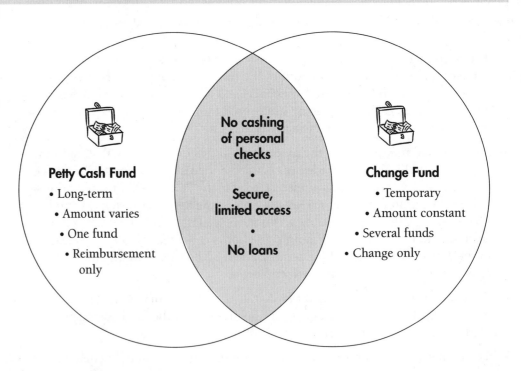

Petty Cash Fund
- Long-term
- Amount varies
- One fund
- Reimbursement only

No cashing of personal checks
•
Secure, limited access
•
No loans

Change Fund
- Temporary
- Amount constant
- Several funds
- Change only

Summary

A petty cash fund offers a convenience to the staff of an active school where many events are ongoing. "Emergency" items of small dollar value can be obtained quickly, without the typical purchase order procedure or the use of the school credit/purchasing card. Be sure, though, to carefully weigh the benefits and disadvantages of maintaining a petty cash fund. Chances are, your school district has strict rules governing the operation of these funds, or it may prohibit their use all together.

If you *do* have a petty cash fund, it is imperative that you and your staff adhere to set procedures. Following the guidelines explained in this chapter can help you protect the fund from theft and misuse, and enable you to enjoy the convenience of quick reimbursement for small, unexpected school purchases. Purchasing that extra extension cord may save the play!

14

Raffles

Raffle—*A type of lottery in which individuals purchase one or more tickets in anticipation of winning an offered prize from a random drawing of tickets. Profits from the sale of prenumbered raffle tickets are used to benefit the entire school, a specific group of students, or the staff. Federal and state regulations applicable to games of chance also apply to school raffles.*

Raffles—particularly ones involving goods and services donated by community businesses—are a popular way for schools to raise money as they generally require less of a time investment than other kinds of fund-raising activities. Some schools raise money for faculty projects by holding raffles for the best parking places in the faculty lot or for season tickets to school events. Other schools hold raffles at school events, such as fairs and banquets, with prizes often donated by members of the business community as tax write-offs. Any profit from a raffle goes to support a school project (e.g., the staff remembrance fund, the general fund, the computer software account). The specific project that will benefit from the raffle should be clear to the ticket buyer at the time of the raffle ticket sale.

While anyone can purchase a ticket for a school raffle, selling tickets involves handling cash and tickets, so carefully weigh the age and maturity of your students before involving them as sellers. If students *do* sell raffle tickets, designate one raffle ticket sales location and require faculty supervision at all times.

As a "game of chance" similar to bingo or an auction, raffles may be subject to state or local restrictions as well as school board policy. Before you proceed with a raffle, consult your school district's guidelines concerning games of chance (e.g., prior approval required from the central accounting office). Your district accounting office will be able to tell you if state regulations apply. It is also important to check with your accounting office to see if there are restrictions on the value and types of prizes you may offer (e.g., no prize worth more than $500; no trip awards on school days).

Furthermore, when raffles are permissible, specific procedures are needed to account for raffle tickets (sold and not sold) and the money collected in order to determine profit or loss. Finally, individuals who win prizes must provide personal information to the school to prevent violation of Internal Revenue Service (IRS) rules. Following the procedures in this chapter will help to ensure proper accounting for raffle-generated funds and compliance with IRS regulations.

Financial Controls for Raffle Ticket Sales

In all cases in which money is collected at school, financial safeguards are needed to ensure that funds are not lost or stolen. Here are some guidelines to follow. (See Figure 14.1 for a graphic summary.)

Electronic ticket boxes can be a great investment. They operate like a cash register by recording the money collected and issuing the purchaser a prenumbered ticket.

- Designate one person to be the raffle coordinator. To maintain a system of checks and balances between receiving funds and preparing deposits, the bookkeeper should *not* serve as a raffle coordinator.

- Use prenumbered raffle tickets to assist in reconciling the money collected to the number of tickets sold. You may also opt to

  – *Use two-part tickets.* The ticket seller gives one part of the ticket to the ticket buyer and retains the other part for the drawing—and for reconciling the money collected with the tickets sold.

  – *Use computerized tickets.* A ticket stub is produced electronically for the buyer, and the sale is recorded in electronic memory.

- Require individual ticket sales reports (see p. 83) to reconcile the number of tickets sold to the amount of money collected.

  – Store the remaining ticket inventory in a locked area with limited key access.

  – Prepare a financial report (see p. 84) at the end of the event to summarize the raffle's receipts and expenses and to determine the profit or loss.

FIGURE **14.1**

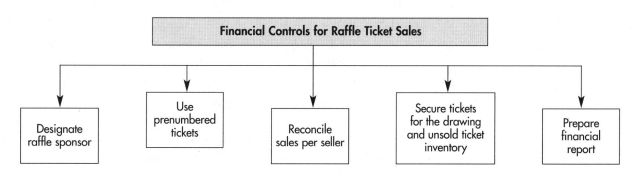

Responsibilities of the Raffle Coordinator

As principal, make sure that the designated raffle coordinator performs the following tasks. (See Figure 14.2 for a graphic summary.)

- Review the individual ticket sales reports completed by each ticket seller.

- Secure the ticket inventory throughout the event to prevent loss or theft of both unsold tickets and the "sold" tickets that will be used in the drawing (e.g., the storage area should be locked with limited key access). To reconcile tickets sold with the money collected, it will be necessary to know the numbers of the first and last raffle tickets sold.

- Secure the funds collected at the end of the day (e.g., forward the money to the bookkeeper for deposit; make a night deposit, if necessary).

- Reconcile ticket sales with the money collected by comparing the total tickets sold on each ticket sales report to the money received.

- Prepare the raffle's financial report and submit it for administrative review.

FIGURE 14.2

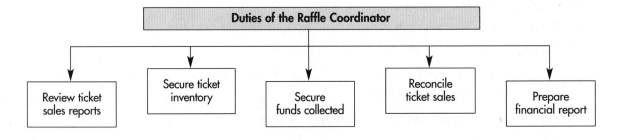

Using a Change Fund

During raffle sales, a change fund is usually necessary to provide ticket buyers with the appropriate change. (See Figure 14.3 for an overview of a change fund's key characteristics.) To start a change fund, write a check from your checking account, coding it to a cash account titled "Change Fund—Raffle." When cashing the check at the bank, be sure to ask for a variety of bills and coins.

Note, though, that access to cash provides an open opportunity for school funds to be lost or misused. The following guidelines will help your school protect a change fund while making it available for the intended purpose.

- Use a change fund *only* to make change; the money is not to be used to reimburse staff for school-related expenditures (University of Virginia, 2002). Never use a change fund to make loans to students and staff or to cash personal checks.

- A change fund is temporary and specific. Do not maintain a change fund in the office for staff to use.

- The amount of the raffle's change fund must remain constant for the duration of the ticket sales period.

- Keep a change fund in a locked box/drawer with compartments for coins and bills; store the box in a locked area with restricted key access. If students are assisting with ticket sales, there should be a supervising faculty member present at all times.

- Rules for using a change fund may vary with each school system, but generally, a change fund used during fund-raising efforts (like a raffle) is deposited back into the school's checking account at the end of the fund-raising activity.

FIGURE 14.3

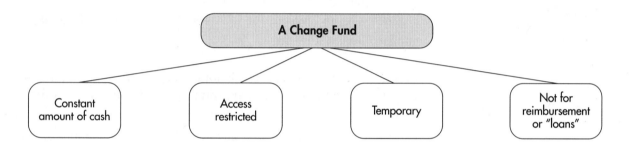

Reporting Raffle Ticket Sales

Each person selling raffle tickets should complete a ticket sales report to reconcile the number of tickets personally sold with the amount of money personally collected. Ticket sellers should record basic information on the form before they begin sales, and then complete the report immediately after their sales shift is over. Please note that this is a *staff,* not a student, responsibility. See Form 14-A for an example of a completed ticket sales report.

FORM 14-A

Raffle Ticket
Sales Report
(see Appendix B, p. 138)

- Just prior to the start of raffle sales, the ticket seller records the color and type of tickets to be sold (e.g., blue tickets for the student government raffle) and the first ticket number available for sale.

- When the ticket sale period ends, the ticket seller calculates* the total number of tickets that he or she has sold. Although the ticket count shown in Form 14-A is easy to determine at a glance, a ticket tally can be more complicated when you don't begin the raffle sale with ticket #1. An easy method is to add "1" to the last ticket number sold. For example, if the tickets sold are numbered from 175 to 184, the number of tickets sold is 10 (i.e., tickets 175, 176, 177, 178, 179, 180, 181, 182, 183, and 184). By adding "1" to 184 (the last ticket sold), the ticket seller gets an accurate count through by simple subtraction (i.e., 185 − 175 = 10 tickets sold).

*If using a computerized form, this and other calculations will be automatic.

- When the tally is complete, the ticket seller calculates the funds by multiplying the cost of the ticket by the number of tickets sold. The sum total of all ticket types should equal the total sales.

- Each ticket seller adds in the amount of his or her portion of the change fund and records the actual amount in the cash box/drawer. Ticket sellers verify the amount of the change fund and sales.

- Finally, the ticket seller signs and dates the completed report and submits it to the raffle coordinator, along with the funds. The raffle coordinator reviews all of the ticket sales reports and either turns the money in to the bookkeeper, or makes a night deposit.

The Raffle Financial Report

The raffle financial report is a summary document. It records the income from the raffle, as reported in individual ticket sales reports; summarizes all expenses related to the raffle; and records the raffle's profit. See Form 14-B for an example of a completed financial report.

FORM **14-B**

Raffle Financial
Report
(see Appendix B, p. 138)

- The raffle coordinator is responsible for completing the financial report. Insist that the report be completed promptly (within one week of the raffle drawing).

- You, as principal, or a designated member of your administrative staff, should review the submitted financial report as soon as possible. If funds or tickets are missing, you will want to know right away.

Taxation Issues

All raffle winnings of monetary value, including non-cash prizes, are subject to federal income tax and must be reported to the IRS.

- Never pay a raffle winner in cash. If the raffle has a monetary prize, the winner should receive a school check for the designated amount.

- As principal of the school, it is your responsibility to inform the raffle winner that all prizes are taxable and must be reported on the individual's income tax return, in accordance with IRS guidelines for reporting prize winnings (see Internal Revenue Service, 2002c). This task is best accomplished by providing the raffle winner with written notification at the time of the award.

- Obtain each raffle winner's name, address, and social security number.

  - If the winnings are more than $600, the school must issue IRS Form W-2G. (Internal Revenue Service, 2002a).
  - If the winnings are more than $5,000, the school district is generally required to withhold federal income taxes (Internal Revenue Service, 2002b).

- For nonmonetary prizes, the winner should report the fair market value of the prize on line 21 of Form 1040, which is labeled "other income." Obtain the fair market value at the time of a prize donation or purchase, and include the information in the written notification given to the raffle winner.

Summary

Raffles and other games of chance are a popular way to raise money because they require a minimum amount of effort. As principal, your job is to review the financial statement with the raffle sponsor as soon as possible after the event. In this way, you can determine that a profit was realized and confirm that all tickets (sold and remaining) have been accounted for. Solve any problems associated with the raffle immediately, and use what you learn from the experience to help eliminate future problems. Also, remember to comply with state and federal government regulations that apply to games of chance. Your district accounting and internal audit departments will be glad to assist you; it is their job to do so.

15

The School Budget

School Budget—*An estimate of the total revenue and expenditures for a school year. The school budget comprises all funds allocated to, and raised by, the school.*

Good budget planning helps ensure that funds are in place to purchase the materials and supplies necessary to support student achievement. Projecting an annual spending plan for your school may seem mysterious or daunting, particularly to a new administrator, but like any administrative skill, it's a process that can be learned.

To project a budget, you need to find out about the sources of your school's funds (i.e., its revenue), and examine past spending patterns (i.e., expenditures). Over time, and with good record keeping, the process will become predictable. This chapter provides the information you need and the steps to follow to develop an annual spending plan for your school.

Revenue Sources

As outlined in Figure 15.1, schools typically receive funds from three sources: (1) the school division's operating budget; (2) grants from companies, organizations, or government agencies; and (3) students, parents, staff, and patrons.

FIGURE 15.1

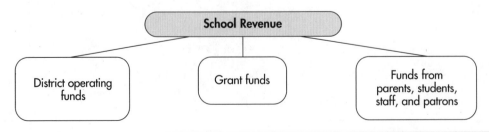

➤ District Operating Funds

Each year, the superintendent and school board develop a new annual operating budget—all the funds needed to keep district schools running for the upcoming year (typically from July 1 to June 30). In addition to setting aside funds to pay for employee salaries and building electricity, districts allocate money to individual schools, which the schools can use to buy equipment and supplies at their own discretion. Although these funds are earmarked for each school, they usually come with spending guidelines. Here is an overview of the typical features of operating funds allocated to individual schools. (See Figure 15.2 for a graphic summary.)

- Operating funds for schools are budgeted in the overall district budget. The money comes from various sources, including local, state, and federal funds.

- Schools typically receive and spend operating funds by category (e.g., office supplies, instructional equipment), with individually numbered accounts established to track these funds. In some school districts, however, operating funds are allocated in blocks and can be spread over several accounts at the principal's discretion. There may also be expenditure limits for individual items within categories (e.g., no equipment item should exceed $500).

- Operating funds are often fund-specific, meaning that money received in one account (e.g., instructional supplies) may not be used to purchase items in another account category (e.g., office equipment). Transfers between accounts may be permissible at certain times of the year, with district permission.

- Operating funds are frequently allocated according to the number of students in the school (e.g., the school receives $5 per student for library supplies).

- Operating funds from district allocations usually have a time limit for spending (e.g., July 1 to April 1). Money left unspent typically reverts to the central office in the late spring. Always spend funds from the central office *first,* before spending other school money! Failure to spend district funds is not a wise budgeting practice (Sielke, 2002). You may be inadvertently sending a message to your district financial officers that you do not need these funds for your school. When given the opportunity, a proactive instructional leader never fails to purchase instructional resources!

FIGURE **15.2**

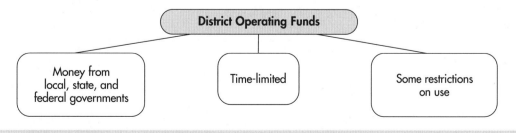

➤ **Grant Funds**

Grant funds are not automatically allocated and usually require a school to file a competitive application with the granting agent (Mutter, 2002). Often, grant funds are *categorical,* meaning that the use of the funds is restricted to certain educational activities, such as staff development, science instruction, or reading remediation. This section provides an overview of the key features of grant funds. (See Figure 15.3 for a graphic summary.)

• Schools receive grant funds from organizations, companies, or government agencies for use in a predetermined project or activity. Schools typically petition for the funds through a written application process.

• Grants usually contain restrictions on how the funds may be used (e.g., grant money cannot be used to pay salaries). Large grants to individual schools (e.g., more than $10,000) may be administered by the district level on the school's behalf. In cases like this, purchases with grant funds are processed at the district level, with items sent to the school. For this reason, some granting agencies will allow the district to charge a small percentage of the grant to cover the "indirect cost" of administering the grant for the school (e.g., accounting and purchasing services).

• Grants have time limits as to when the funds may be spent.

• Grants differ in the way funds are given to the school. Some allocations are *up-front grants,* meaning the funds are paid to the school or district in installments before expenditures are made; other grants are *reimbursement grants,* meaning that the school spends its own money first and is later reimbursed by the granting agent.

• Grants provide directions on any reporting requirements, which may include informing the granting agent of the funded project's time line and results.

• School-level grants from state and local agencies are becoming increasingly available, because of the national standards movement.

FIGURE **15.3**

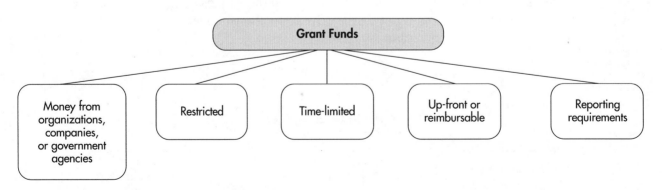

➤ Funds from Parents, Students, Staff, and Patrons

Each year, schools take in a variety of funds from parents, students, staff, and patrons through ticket sales to school events, vending machines, the school store, field trip fees, supplementary supply fees, and numerous club-related fund-raising activities. All of the money that comes to your school in this manner is placed in one of many possible accounts, according to the school activity it is intended to support (hence the name "school activity" funds). For example, money collected from parents for a field trip is placed in a field trip account. Money collected from school community members for tickets to a senior play is placed in the drama club account. As highlighted in Chapter 4, activity funds are unique public educational funds because they are spent directly at the school level by the principal on behalf of students. There are three categories of activity funds:

- *School accounts* contain money used to pay for the educational resources your school needs (e.g., general fund, English supplies). Some of these funds (e.g., instructional and office supplies) may come annually from your district's central office. Grant funds paid directly to the school are also allocated to school accounts.
- *Student accounts* contain money raised by students (e.g., sale of bumper stickers by the student government) for use by the specific student group that raised the funds or by the student body as a whole.
- *Flow-through accounts* contain money collected at the school on behalf of the central office or another program (e.g., summer school funds). These funds are not available for your school program and must be forwarded to the central office at the appropriate time.

Here is an overview of the key features of activity funds raised by your school community through means such as ticket sales to events, field trips, vending machines, and club projects. (See Figure 15.4 for a graphic summary.)

- Funds generated in this way are restricted in use (e.g., field trip funds are restricted to field trip expenditures).

- Accounts funded by students legally belong to the students in the organization that raised the funds (Thompson & Wood, 1998). For this reason, activity funds should benefit the group who generated the funds; these funds should not be spent for other purposes without written permission from your district.

- School activity funds raised by your school community do not have a time limit for expenditures; however, it's a good goal to spend most of these funds within the same school year. Any balance in an activity fund "rolls over" for use in the next school year.

- School activity funds are accounted for separately from funds raised by parent organizations, such as band parents and booster clubs. (See Chapter 12: Parent Organizations.)

- Activity funds have reporting and annual audit requirements, as specified within your district and state guidelines (see Chapter 18: Surviving an Audit).

Aim to spend approximately 90 percent of school activity funds during the year those funds were raised.

FIGURE **15.4**

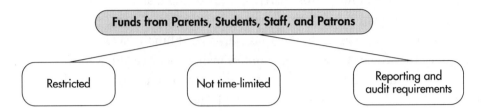

Projecting the Annual School Budget

Each year's budget is reasonably predictable in terms of both revenue (i.e., money coming in) and expenditures (i.e., money going out). As principal, you need to prepare budget projections for school activity accounts funded by the central office to help operate the school and those funds raised at the school. However, there are a couple of exceptions:

– Because the funds in *student accounts* (e.g., club accounts) are typically spent in the same year those funds are raised, it's not strictly necessary to project a budget for these accounts. However, you may wish to work with student sponsors to get an idea of spending plans, particularly if the students are very young. (All the money should not be spent on pizza parties!) Because athletics often generate a large amount of annual revenue, be sure to meet with your athletic director to help ensure wise spending.

– Because *flow-through accounts* (e.g., lost and damaged textbook fees) are forwarded to the central office each year, there is no need to project a budget for these accounts.

– Budgets for grants are developed at the time of grant applications and are revised according to the granting body's specified guidelines.

• A basic principle of projecting a budget for your school activity accounts is that the past is the best predictor of the future (Mutter, 2002). When new to a school, compile a three-year history for each expenditure account (e.g., office supplies, science supplies). Meet with the bookkeeper and ask the following questions:

– How much was spent in this account in each of the past three years?

– How much money was received for this account over the past three years?

– Were there any atypical expenses in the past three years that may have altered this account's usual spending patterns (e.g., the purchase of a school gift, expenses related to hosting the regional science fair)?

– What is the balance in this account after all current and outstanding bills have been paid?

Allow the bookkeeper sufficient time to compile the current balance and history of each account.

- Once you have the account balances, calculate the *average yearly revenue* of each account over the past three years. (For example, if the computer software/supplies account had revenue allocations of $1,055, $951, and $1,146, its three-year average yearly revenue would be $1,051.) If your district office's allocation figures for the upcoming school year are available to you, use these figures as the "fourth year" and calculate four-year averages.

- Now determine the likely amount that will be available to spend for the upcoming year by adding the account's average yearly revenue figure to the account's current balance, which will "roll over" to the next school year. (To continue with the computer software/supplies account example, you would add the average yearly revenue of $1,051 to the current account balance of $321 to arrive at a figure of $1,372.) For each account, enter the resulting figures as your initial estimate of the funds available for spending, assuming no change in allocation factors, such as your school's enrollment.

- Next, calculate the *average yearly expenditures* of each account over the past three years (e.g., $960 + $850 + $1,200 = $1,003). The resulting figures provide a reasonable estimate of what will be spent in each account for the upcoming year, providing that spending patterns remain the same. You may need to adjust these average-based estimates to account for atypical expenses in the past and for future spending plans. The advice of veteran teachers and administrative staff will help with this task.

- With your bookkeeper, establish expenditure and revenue targets for each account. This exercise is best done during the summer months, at the beginning of the annual funding period or fiscal year (e.g., July 1 to June 30). Throughout the year, revisit each account regularly (e.g., quarterly) to ensure that the school remains within the projected budget and to make appropriate adjustments.

- Throughout the school year, ask your bookkeeper to provide you with monthly status summaries of your school accounts. As principal, you should know as much about available funds as your bookkeeper does.

- Once you are experienced in the school, maintain a five-year history of each account to establish the annual budget. This process is easily done with the use of electronic spreadsheets, and you'll find that, with practice, it will take less and less of your time.

tip

An average may over- or underestimate expenditures, but it is an excellent starting point.

Summary

In projecting a school budget, remember that recent past history is a good predictor of future school revenue and likely expenditures. Use available past records of spending in each account, and remember to seek the advice of experienced staff members, including teachers as well as the bookkeeper. Boldly develop a spending plan for the year, and then revisit it at least quarterly to see if projections are on target or if you need to make revisions. Finally, always remember that the money in your school is there to benefit teaching and learning; spend it wisely, but *do* spend it.

16

The School Store

School Store—*A school-operated store where student supplies are sold. The inventory volume and types of items available are based on school board procedures and the student population (e.g., gym suits for middle and high schools, pencils for elementary schools).*

School stores provide a convenient service to students and staff and an opportunity for the school to make a modest profit. They can also be an excellent opportunity for older students to learn valuable lessons in business and economics. However, if proper staffing, inventory, and deposit procedures are not followed, a school store can become an opportunity for theft and loss of school property.

As principal, you need to know the basic principles and safeguards related to school store operation, particularly if you are new to the school. The response that "we have always done it this way" may not be enough to prevent items and money from disappearing in unauthorized ways. This chapter describes the procedures necessary to ensure that your school store runs efficiently and that store items and profits are protected from loss, damage, and theft.

Establishing a School Store

This section assumes that your school is currently not operating a store but is interested in starting one. Here is an overview of the steps to follow. (See Figure 16.1 for a graphic summary.)

- Designate several staff members to review any applicable district guidelines and decide the items to be sold in the store. These individuals should identify the types of items and the price range of the merchandise.

- Establish a maximum dollar limit for the store inventory (e.g., an elementary store should never have more than $500 in inventory).

- Check with other principals to find out which supply vendors offer the best deals on merchandise. Remember that item prices affect the store's profit margin.

- Select a staff member to be responsible for the store's daily operations. The school store sponsor should be someone other than the bookkeeper (e.g., a teacher or teacher assistant). Separation of duties provides for more internal control: the person receiving money from the store should *not* be the same person who is accounting for funds and making deposits.

- Create a change fund by writing a check and coding it to a cash account titled "Change Fund—School Store."

- Establish the hours of operation.

- Designate a secure location for the school store and overflow inventory storage. The store should be locked when not in operation, and access to the key should be restricted.

- Review your district's procedure for tracking consumable inventory items with the store sponsor. At a minimum, follow district guidelines.

Remember that the goal of a school store is to provide a credible school service, not to realize a big profit with "cheap" items and high prices.

FIGURE 16.1

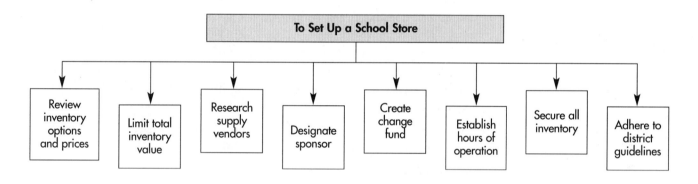

School Store Operations

In the subsections that follow, we provide an overview of school store operations, focusing on the duties of the store sponsor and the bookkeeper.

➤ Receipting Procedures

- At the end of each day, the store sponsor prepares one receipt for the money collected that day or prints a cash register list of daily sales (see Chapter 9: Fund-Raising Events, for a sample individual receipt).

- The school sponsor gives the bookkeeper the store receipt or cash register tape, the financial envelope, and the money collected. The bookkeeper, in turn, issues a receipt to the store sponsor for the money received. The money is then included in the daily bank deposit.

➤ Purchasing Store Merchandise to Sell

- The store sponsor prepares and submits a purchase order request to buy items for the store to you, the principal, for approval.

Purchases to stock the school store should follow standard purchasing procedure.

• The bookkeeper prepares the purchase order, using the approved purchase requisition.

➤ Receiving Vendor Merchandise and Stocking the Store

• The store sponsor receives the merchandise, signs the packing slip, and stocks the school store.

• The bookkeeper pays for merchandise based on the purchase order, the invoice, and the (sponsor-signed) packing slip.

➤ Conducting a Physical Inventory

• All physical counts of merchandise should involve both the store sponsor and a second staff member—someone other than bookkeeper.

• Count the full inventory at least once at the end of each fiscal year (usually June 30). Perform quarterly "spot checks" of highly desirable items. We also recommend counting the full inventory before a new staff member assumes responsibility for the store's daily operations.

FORM 16-A

School Store Physical Inventory Report
(see Appendix B, p. 139)

• When counting the inventory, use a format similar to Form 16-A. Provide a description of inventory items, list the number of items on hand, and record the purchase price to determine the available stock and the value of the ending inventory. Both the school store sponsor and the "second staff member" should sign and date the completed form.

➤ Selecting and Supervising Student Workers

• Use responsible students to assist with the store (e.g., to make change) when appropriate for age and level of responsibility; rotate workers monthly to prevent overdependence on one or two students.

• Arrange for an adult to be on duty when students are assisting in the school store, and count the change fund daily.

• Conduct "spot" inventories of highly desirable items every three months to help deter theft.

Using a Change Fund

Keep a controlled change fund to provide the appropriate change to school store patrons. (See Figure 16.2 for an overview of a change fund's key characteristics.) Access to cash provides an open opportunity for school funds to be lost or misused. The following guidelines will allow your school to protect a change fund, while making it available for its intended use.

• Use a change fund *only* to make change; the money is not to be used to reimburse staff for school-related expenditures (University of Virginia, 2002). Never use a change fund to make loans to students and staff or to cash personal checks.

• The actual amount of a change fund must remain constant throughout a fund's duration. For example, it might be appropriate to maintain a change fund of $10 for an elementary school store and $50 for a secondary school store. Count the change fund daily. "Refresh" the fund with smaller bills and coins from the bank as needed.

- Keep the school store's change fund (when not in use) in a locked box or drawer with compartments for coins and bills; store the box in a locked area with restricted key access. Periodically, ask someone other than the store sponsor to count the change fund.

- Rules for using a change fund may vary with each school system, but generally, a change fund for a school store is deposited into your checking account at the end of the school year.

FIGURE **16.2**

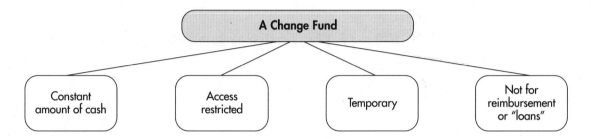

The School Store's Profitability

Review the annual profit of your school store to determine if it is reasonable.

- School stores typically generate profit in the 10–20 percent range. To determine your school store's annual profit, follow these easy steps:

  - Subtract the value of the in-stock inventory from the balance in the "School Store" account. (See Form 16-A.) If the fund balance for the school store is $740 (assuming that all bills are paid), and the value of the in-stock inventory is $580, the profit is $160 ($740 – $580).
  - To determine the percentage of profit, divide the profit ($160) by the fund balance ($740) and multiply by 100.

- At the end of the fiscal year (June 30), transfer the *profit* from the school store (e.g., $160) to the school's general fund. The balance remaining in the "School Store" fund account now equals the value of the available inventory to be sold in the new school year.

Summary

The operation of a school store can provide a convenient service to members of the school community and an opportunity for modest profit and valuable lessons. As principal, you should be familiar with the procedures to operate your school store safely and efficiently. By following the basic principles of operation, separation of duties, and inventory control explained in this chapter, you can prevent the store from becoming an easy target for staff or student theft.

17

Staff Reimbursement

Staff Reimbursement—
The process of paying-back staff for approved expenses incurred on behalf of the school (e.g., purchase of school supplies or travel expenses). District guidelines usually determine both the maximum dollar amount that can be reimbursed at the school level and the procedures to follow.

The process of reimbursing school staff for expenditures can be frustrating for the principal and the bookkeeper if clear procedures are not in place, enforced, and known to all. To avoid problems—such as well-intentioned staff who "buy now and ask later" and unexpected bills for which funds are unavailable—require staff to obtain written authorization before spending school funds. No one should make school-related purchases on the assumption that approval will be granted afterward. Verbal consent as part of a discussion in the hallway is not a substitute for written approval. This chapter explains procedures for handling monetary reimbursements to staff so that everyone is happy with the outcome.

Reimbursing Staff for Materials and Supplies

The information in this section describes how to repay a staff member who is personally paying for supply items on behalf of the school. Figure 17.1 provides a graphic summary of the major points applicable to you, the principal.

FORM 17-A

Purchase Order
(Staff Reimbursement Use)
(see Appendix B, p. 139)

- Insist that all staff members' requests for reimbursement be preceded by an approved and signed purchase order (see Form 17-A for an example).

- In cases where a staff member is picking up small amounts of supplies, such as food items or decorations that are not typically delivered by a vendor, issue a prenumbered, in-house purchase order in the staff member's name. This form can serve as a "blanket purchase order" for a school event (e.g., school dance, school fair) where a number of small, unanticipated expenses may surface.

- In cases where the district office or PTA allots each teacher a certain amount to spend on classroom supplies, a blanket purchase order for that amount (signed and dated by you, the principal) can be written in the name of each teacher on July 1. Teachers can then "buy against" the approved order throughout the summer and school year until they reach the allotted dollar limit.

- Be sure to follow district and state regulations with regard to allowable dollar limits for purchase orders issued at the school level (e.g., the district might have a dollar limit of $500).

- Specify the "not-to-exceed" dollar amount (e.g., $25) and the type of items to be purchased (e.g., food supplies, office supplies) before signing the purchase order. Include the school's tax exempt number.

- Make sure that staff members who are buying items at a store know to present the purchase order to the vendor (i.e., the sales clerk) at the time of payment, so that sales tax on the purchase can be waived. Schools are nonprofit organizations and, therefore, tax exempt.

- Instruct teachers to attach the vendor's receipt and related packing slip to the purchase order, and forward these documents to the bookkeeper.

- Issue a check to the staff member from the appropriate fund account (e.g., Smile Club, student government). Never reimburse in cash. (For information on how to establish and account for a petty cash fund, see Chapter 13: The Petty Cash Fund.)

- Be sure your bookkeeper files all documentation with the purchase order.

- Distribute written spending procedures on how to obtain reimbursement for material and supply expenses to your staff at the beginning of the school year and be sure to give this information to all new personnel who arrive during the year.

- Be consistent with all staff members; those who violate the established purchasing procedures repeatedly will stop doing so when they have to bear the expenses personally.

tip

Auditors look for purchase orders that were dated after a purchase was made. This is a clear violation of standard purchasing procedure and may negatively affect your audit report.

FIGURE **17.1**

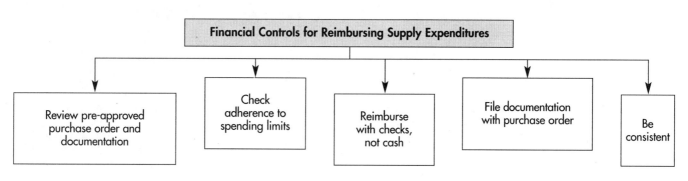

Reimbursing School-Related Travel Expenses

This section explains how to authorize and reimburse a staff member for expenses incurred during out-of-town travel that benefits the school. (See Figure 17.2 for a graphic summary.)

- Pre-approve staff members' out-of-town travel with a signed, district travel expense form or an alternative, like Form 17-A.

    – Authorize school-funded travel only for out-of-town trips that clearly benefit the school. Remember, no one should approve his or her own travel—not even you, as the principal. If you are planning a school-related trip, ask an authorized central office administrator for approval.

    – At school, an immediate supervisor should approve the estimated travel expenses before a trip (Georgetown University, 2002).

    – If local travel is part of the job description (e.g., the bookkeeper's trips to the bank), follow district guidelines regarding procedures and eligibility for mileage reimbursement.

- As soon as the travel is approved, encumber (obligate or set aside) the funds in the appropriate fund account (e.g., staff development, teacher conferences). Once you have authorized reimbursement, the bookkeeper enters the actual expenses and issues the reimbursement check. By tracking travel expenses in this manner, you can ensure that these expenses are not reimbursed more than once.

- Require documentation. Within a week of the trip's conclusion, the traveler should complete and submit an itemized travel expense form (see Form 17-B) for administrative review.

- Be consistent in reimbursing for travel. When a travel expense form is submitted, evaluate the reimbursement requests based on district guidelines for meal expenses, daily spending limits, mileage, and purchase of alcohol (usually not permitted). Note that travel expenses incurred by family members (e.g., the coach's wife) are *not* eligible for reimbursement.

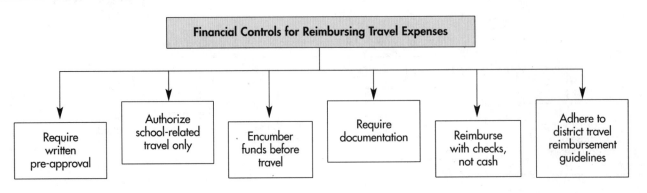

tip

Always be prudent when traveling at the public's expense. The Freedom of Information Act allows anyone to access travel expenses for public employees.

FORM **17-B**

Travel Expense Form
(see Appendix B,
pp. 140–141)

FIGURE **17.2**

Financial Controls for Reimbursing Travel Expenses

Require written pre-approval

Authorize school-related travel only

Encumber funds before travel

Require documentation

Reimburse with checks, not cash

Adhere to district travel reimbursement guidelines

Travel Advances

Occasions may arise when a staff member wants or needs money to cover costs related to an upcoming, authorized school trip. Although expensive trips that require travel advances should be infrequent, this section explains how to handle the details so that problems do not occur.

- Permit travel advances for out-of-town travel only. Require travelers to submit a travel advance form (see Form 17-C) for your (or your designee's) review and authorization.

  - This form should indicate the amount of money requested, the reason for the trip, the trip destination, and the trip date. It should also include space for the traveler's and the authorizing administrator's signature.
  - No one should approve his or her own travel advance. If you, the principal, need a travel advance, ask an appropriate central office administrator to authorize payment from school funds.

- Establish written procedures that explain (1) how long a travel advance may be held before a trip and (2) how long the traveler may wait before turning in the final expense form (e.g., five working days after the trip). The traveler's signature on the travel advance form indicates that he or she understands the "rules" pertaining to travel advances.

- Reconcile final travel expenses once the trip is over by comparing the amount of the travel advance to the actual cost of the trip, as documented on the employee's itemized travel expense form (see Form 17-B). If the trip costs less than the advance, the traveler pays the difference to the school in the form of a personal check.

- Prohibit new travel advances until the traveler has cleared all prior advances through you and your bookkeeper.

Summary

Providing clear, written procedures for reimbursing school staff for legitimate expenditures will save everyone time in the busy business of schooling. Help staff to understand that creating an easy-to-follow paper trail for all expenditures protects everyone who spends school money. This protection is particularly important when public funds are used to reimburse staff members for the purchase of items or travel expenses. To maintain the trust of the community and the public at large, school staff must avoid even the appearance of impropriety. Equally important, advance approval of expenditures allows you to ensure that funds are available and, thus, prevent deficit accounts.

FORM **17-C**

Travel Advance
Form
(see Appendix B, p. 141)

18

Surviving an Audit

A school audit is typically an independent assessment of the school's financial health. An independent auditor or team samples financial records and renders an opinion about (1) whether or not bookkeeping records accurately reflect the financial activity of the school for a designated period and (2) whether or not sound business practices are being used. An audit can also encompass "performance" measures to assess the overall operation of a program and determine if a school's financial resources are being used appropriately.

All audits begin with objectives, and these objectives determine the type of audit to be conducted and the audit standards to be followed (U.S. General Accounting Office, 1999). Audits can be either *internal* (i.e., conducted by employees of the school system, city, or state) or *external* (i.e., conducted by outside professionals, such as CPA firms). Overall, the purpose of an audit is to reassure the school's administration, district officers, school board, and taxpayers that a school is handling its funds according to generally accepted business procedures.

The Roles of Internal Auditors and External Auditors

Both internal and external auditors review a sample of your school financial records carefully, but they tend to do so from different perspectives. Figure 18.1 contrasts the roles of internal and external auditors (Sawyer, Dittenhofer, & Scheiner, 1996).

Both types of auditors are professionally educated in accounting and auditing standards. If your school district has a staff of internal auditors, they will probably visit your school more than once a year, and you will get to know them on a personal basis. Ask for their advice and invite them in for additional reviews if you have any concerns regarding your office staff. They can help increase your level of confidence in handling school money matters.

FIGURE **18.1**

Comparison of Internal Auditors and External Auditors

Internal Auditors	External Auditors
Employees of the school system	Independent service providers
Independent of the activities audited, but responsive to the needs and wishes of the school/district administration and the school board	Independent of the school/district administration and the school board, both in fact and attitude
Directly concerned with the prevention of fraud	Incidentally concerned with the prevention and detection of fraud, but directly concerned when financial statements are substantially affected
Reviews financial activities on an ongoing basis	Reviews financial records periodically, usually once a year

The Audit Team's Tools

• An audit usually begins with auditors asking you and your bookkeeper to complete an *internal control questionnaire.*

  – This document consists of a number of questions about the bookkeeping procedures currently used at your school (e.g., Are individual receipts written for collected amounts above $3? Are school store receipts forwarded to the bookkeeper daily?). These questions are based on the policies and procedures required by your school district (Sawyer, Dittenhofer, & Scheiner, 1996).
  – By reviewing the questionnaire, the auditors get initial insight into whether your school is actually using the policies and procedures set by your district office and school board.
  – You and your bookkeeper should answer each question on the internal control questionnaire completely and truthfully. Hiding areas of ignorance, confusion, or concern from the audit team benefits no one. Although a poor audit may temporarily affect your professional career, deceptive behavior may have greater long-term consequences. Corrective strategies, implemented over time by you and your bookkeeper, usually take care of accounting problems.

• Auditors often use *audit software,* which provides a number of useful tools, including

  – Statistical sampling programs, which randomly select a sample of records (e.g., purchase orders, checks, or bank statements) to be included in the audit, based on auditor specifications.

Your audit will be based on state or district written procedures pertaining to activity funds. Find these documents, read them, and use them.

– Flowcharting programs (e.g. allCLEAR), which graphically display book-keeping procedures.

– Data analysis programs, which extract data that meet predetermined criteria (e.g., list of checks where payment exceeds $600).

- Once the auditors have selected a sample set of documents from your book-keeping records, they apply *standards and professional judgment* to determine the overall audit result. The audit team bases its evaluation on your school's bookkeeping procedures, on state or district and school board policies, and on professional standards, such as the U.S. General Accounting Office's *Government Auditing Standards* (1999), the Institute of Internal Auditors' *Standards for Professional Practice of Internal Auditing* (2003), and the Financial Accounting Standards Board's "Generally Accepted Accounting Principles" (GAAP).

What Auditors Review and What They Look For

When auditors visit your school, they are likely to review a number of the financial tasks handled by your bookkeeper and teachers (e.g., checks written, receipts issued, purchase orders processed) over a specific period of time (e.g., July 1 to October 30). Figure 18.2 provides an overview of the audit team's areas of interest. Advance knowledge of what the audit team is likely to look for and, more importantly, why the team will be asking certain questions and reviewing certain documents will help you ensure great audit reports for your school.

FIGURE **18.2**

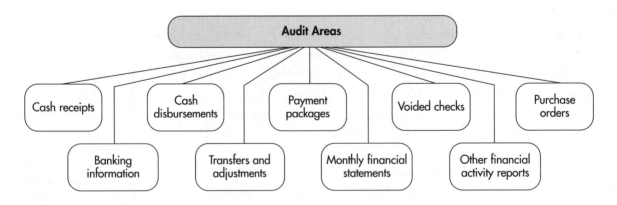

➤ Cash Receipts

Because the handling of the money coming into your school is a major financial responsibility of your bookkeeper, auditors examine several documents related to cash receipts.

- Auditors are likely to request your *cash receipts journal*—a (usually) computerized bookkeeping record of the office receipts issued for a given time period. Typically, the cash receipts journal includes (1) the date of the receipt;

(2) the receipt number; (3) the name of the person issued the receipt
(i.e., who brought money to the bookkeeper); (4) the dollar amount of the
receipt; and (5) the activity fund account (e.g., school pictures, student government, athletic fund) that was increased. Auditors examine the cash receipts
journal to confirm the following:

- Office receipts were issued in numerical order and there are no missing
  receipt numbers.
- The name of the person who issued receipts to students and the amount of
  money forwarded to the bookkeeper.
- Teacher/sponsor-issued receipts match the bookkeeper's office receipts.
  (This helps the auditors to verify that funds were submitted to the office
  every day.)
- Receipts were posted to the computerized system correctly (e.g., fund-
  raising receipts were posted to the fund-raising account).
- The bookkeeper issued daily receipts for all money received in the office,
  these receipts were issued to the actual teacher/sponsor who collected
  the funds, and the amount of the receipts equals the total of the money
  collected by the teacher/sponsor.

Auditors use the cash receipts journal to select a sample of office receipts to
review in further detail. For example, they might compare the office receipts
with teacher receipts issued and with the money deposited in the bank.

- The audit team may examine teacher/sponsor-issued receipts to verify that the
  money collected was receipted to the students or parents and that all money
  was forwarded daily to the bookkeeper. They also confirm that the dates and
  amounts on teacher/sponsor receipts match those on the office receipts issued
  and the bank deposits records.

- Auditors also look carefully at all voided receipts (teacher/sponsor and office)
  to confirm the following:

  - All copies of voided teacher/sponsor receipts are present in the teacher/
    sponsor's receipt book (i.e., if the school uses a three-part receipt, all three
    copies of the receipt are available).
  - All voided office receipts are available for review.
  - The bookkeeper included the reason for the void (e.g., issued to the wrong
    teacher) on each voided office receipt.
  - The bookkeeper voided office receipts sparingly—only when an error could
    not be corrected through an adjustment. (See Chapter 19: Transfers and
    Adjustments.)

➤ Cash Disbursements

The handling of money going out of your school is another major responsibility
of your bookkeeper.

- Auditors are likely to request a copy of your *cash disbursement journal* for the
  period under review. A cash disbursement journal is a (usually) computerized

bookkeeping report that provides (1) a chronological listing of the date a check was written, (2) the check number, (3) the name of the person or company being paid, (4) the dollar amount of the check, and (5) the activity fund account that was reduced by the payment. Auditors examine the cash receipts journal to confirm the following:

– All checks were issued in numerical order.

– There are no missing checks.

– Disbursements by check were posted to the right account code and in the right amount.

The auditors also use the records in the cash disbursement journal to assemble a list of individuals and vendors that were paid during the specified audit period.

➤ Payment Packages

Once auditors have selected a sample group of vendors that have received payment, they review all supporting documentation for each payment. This documentation is often referred to as the *payment package*. Each payment package should include (1) either a copy of the check or the computerized check stub, (2) the vendor invoice or original store receipt, (3) the purchase order, and (4) receiving documents from the packaging that show the school received the merchandise.

• Auditors examine checks in payment packages to confirm the following:

– All checks issued were posted correctly to the computerized system or, in the case of manual checks, all checks were entered correctly into the computerized bookkeeping system.

– The bookkeeper issued a check for all funds disbursed (except for payments from a petty cash fund; see Chapter 13: The Petty Cash Fund for more information).

– All checks were issued to the same company/person indicated and approved on the purchase order.

– The payment was accompanied by an approved purchase order.

– All vendor invoices and store receipts are original documents (i.e., no copies).

– All purchases took place after the purchase order was approved (i.e., no orders were placed before the principal approved the purchase order).

– The account from which the funds were paid had a balance equal to or greater than the purchase amount (i.e., the fund account did not have a negative balance before or after the purchase).

– The amount of each purchase was equal to or less than the amount that was approved, and the proper fund account was decreased by the amount of the expenditure.

• Auditors review payments to individuals and privately owned companies (i.e., companies that are not incorporated) for services provided, to confirm that your school sent copies of the payment checks to your district office. The IRS requires organizations to complete and file a Form 1099-MISC when payments to an individual or privately owned company exceed $600 in any calendar year (Internal Revenue Service, 2002a). This guideline applies to payments issued by your school district as a whole, not just those issued by your school.

➤ Voided Checks

Auditors verify that all voided checks are available for review. They also verify that all voided checks have been defaced (e.g., the signature line has been removed; see Chapter 1: Activity Fund Safeguards).

➤ Purchase Orders

Your school orders many items during the course of a year. At some point during an audit, the auditors will want to verify that purchase orders were issued in accordance with procurement guidelines established by the state, city, county, and school board.

- Auditors may examine vendors payments that exceeded established purchase-order dollar limits to ensure that your school followed the required procedures for when to complete bids and price quotes.

- Auditors are likely to focus on your *purchase order status report,* a (usually) computerized bookkeeping report that includes (1) the date the purchase order was issued, (2) the purchase order number, (3) the name of the person or company issued the purchase order, (4) the fund account that was charged with the encumbrance (i.e., the estimated amount of the purchase, used to set aside funds), and (5) the actual purchase order amount. When reviewing this report, auditors seek to confirm the following:

  – Purchase orders were issued in numerical order.
  – There are no missing purchase order numbers.
  – All issued purchase orders were approved by the principal.
  – At the time of approval, the fund account to be charged for the expenditure had a balance sufficient to cover the expenditure.
  – All vendors received payment.

- Auditors may review unfilled or "open" purchase orders to ensure that your school does not have purchase orders for items that will no longer be honored (i.e., purchase orders where orders were canceled).

- Auditors review a copy of purchase orders issued or paid during the audit period (i.e., the auditors may ask to see a purchase order that was issued in a previous period but paid during the current audit period). They are attempting to verify that all purchase orders were issued in accordance with purchasing guidelines (e.g., the dollar amount of the invoice was equal to or less than the purchase order; the purchase order was pre-approved by the principal).

➤ Banking Information

Your banking records reveal a great deal about how your school handles financial matters. As a consequence, auditors are very interested in (1) the monthly bank statements that are issued for your school's checking and saving accounts, (2) the reconciliation of bank statements to your bookkeeping records, and (3) the deposit slips processed by the bank for the selected audit period (e.g., July to

tip

Always deface and save voided checks.

June). Continued problems with bank reconciliations may indicate incompetence or fraud on the part of your staff.

Bank statements

Auditors review the monthly bank statements for all accounts. Each monthly checking account statement includes the canceled (i.e., cleared) checks and deposits that were processed by the bank, as well as your overall and daily account balances.

- Auditors review cleared checks to confirm the following:
  - All school signature procedures were followed (e.g., each check has two signatures; employees did not sign checks payable to themselves).
  - The endorsement of the company and/or person who received each check matches the name listed on the check.
  - No checks were altered.

- Auditors review all deposits processed by all banks to ensure that the deposits were made in a timely manner and that the amount of all deposits equals the amount of receipts processed by the school.

- Auditors review each bank account's records to ensure that its daily balance never exceeded the $100,000 limit for insurance, as established by the Federal Deposit Insurance Corporation (FDIC). Exceeding this limit is an unnecessary school risk.

- Most auditors also question large service charges, school errors on deposit slips, "stop payments" on checks, and checks that were returned due to non-sufficient funds (NSF).

Reconciliations of bank statements

Auditors expect to see that all monthly bank statements during the audit period (e.g., July to June) have been properly reconciled with the balance shown in the bookkeeping system for checking and savings accounts. They examine reconciliation documents to confirm the following:

- All reconciliations of bank statements with the school's monthly financial statements were prepared correctly. (See Chapter 3: Bank Reconciliation.)
- Bank charges (e.g., service charges) were recorded in the school's bookkeeping records correctly each month.
- The principal approved the reconciliation of the monthly bank statements.

Deposit slips

The daily deposit slips that were processed by the bank (i.e., stamped by the bank with the amount, date, time, and account number of deposit) should be available for the auditors to review. It is important that auditors be able to verify that deposits tie back directly to money received at the school.

- Auditors compare date, time, amount, and account number of daily deposit slips to the deposits recorded in the school's bookkeeping records. They match these documents to office receipts issued by the bookkeeper to ensure that your school is not violating district guidelines by keeping funds in the building overnight or over weekends.

- Auditors look for partial deposits (i.e., where the receipts for the day exceed the deposit amount). A pattern of partial receipts could be an indication that the bookkeeper is "lapping receipts," which means that receipts are issued for money received, but the money is not deposited until a future date, allowing for personal use the of funds during the time it is "borrowed" (Robertson, 2000).

➤ Transfers and Adjustments

Auditors are likely to request your *transfers and adjustments journal*. This is a computerized report that indicates (1) the date of the transaction, (2) the number of the transfer or adjustment, (3) the accounts that were increased and or decreased, and (4) the dollar amount of each transaction. When examining the transfers and adjustments journal, auditors look to confirm the following:

- There are no "missing" transfers and adjustments.
- All transfer and adjustment forms were completed in numerical order.
- All transfers and adjustments were posted correctly and approved by an authorized individual.

Typically, the auditors review either all or a sample of the transfers and adjustments posted during the audit period.

➤ Monthly Financial Statements

Auditors want to review your *monthly financial statements* for the audit period. This report includes a list of major activity fund accounts (e.g., field trips, fund-raising events) and the status of each, including (1) the beginning balance of each account or group of accounts (e.g., total of all field trips, fund-raising events), (2) the dollar amount of receipts posted to each account group, (3) the dollar amount of checks written and posted to each account group, (4) the dollar amount of transfers and adjustments posted, and (5) the ending balance of each account.

- The details of all transactions listed in a monthly financial statement are reported by individual account in other documents (e.g., general ledger, cash receipts journal, cash disbursements journal).

- In general, auditors review the financial report for reasonableness (e.g., are the school's receipts and expenditures similar to prior years?). They look for accounts with negative balances and at the school's overall financial position (i.e., balance in the student accounts, school accounts, and flow-through accounts). (See Chapter 4: Bookkeeping Basics, for more information on types of accounts.)

➤ Other Financial Activity Reports and Information

Auditors may request a sampling of other reports pertaining to your school's financial operations.

Athletic event financial reports

Any ticket sales event may be subject to audit, but athletic events are major sources of school revenue and are, therefore, of special interest to auditors. Auditors examine the financial statements from each game, reports of ticket sales, and remaining ticket inventory.

- Auditors are interested in verifying that financial reports are correct by comparing the information on file to the receipts issued, deposits made, and checks written.

- Auditors also seek confirmation that your school has followed IRS guidelines for paying school or city employees for their work at school athletic events. (See Chapter 2: Admission Tickets, for further information.)

Field trip applications and financial reports

Auditors usually review a sample of field trip applications to confirm the following:

- Each trip was within school board policy (e.g., must add educational value).
- Each trip was approved by the principal before money was collected from students and before financial commitments were made (e.g., the bus company was not reserved before the field trip was approved).
- All students who paid to go on the field trip (plus any students listed as unable to pay) actually went on the trip.
- Students did not bear any staff member or chaperone expenses.

Fund-raising permits and fund-raising financial reports

- Auditors review fund-raising authorizations to ensure that each fund-raising event was approved by you, the principal, prior to money being collected and before the commitment was made to a vendor to purchase items for sale (e.g., candy was not ordered before the permit was approved).

- Auditors review fund-raising event financial reports to ensure that the money collected was equal to the number of items purchased after unsold inventory was subtracted (e.g., 100 candy bars were sold at $1 each, and $100 was receipted).

- Auditors review school checks written to ensure that you, the principal, approved these purchases and that the purchases were appropriate (e.g., staff members did not benefit from student fund-raising profits).

- Auditors review the profit percentage for each fund-raising event to see if it is close to the amount that was anticipated. (See Chapter 9: Fund-Raising Events, for further information.)

School store profit and inventory reports

The school store may be audited in detail, depending on the dollar value of its sales and inventory.

- Auditors check to see that the school has conducted at least one physical count of the inventory each school year (more if the dollar value and quantity of inventory are high). If the dollar value of the school store inventory is significant, then the auditors may perform a detailed spot-check of stocked items; otherwise, the auditors may only verify that the inventory procedures are adequate.

- If the auditors determine that the school store's internal controls (i.e., safeguards) are not adequate, they may review receipting practices from the office, checks written, and inventory records. Such a review may also include verification of the dollar amount of the total inventory and annual store profit. (See Chapter 16: The School Store, for further information.)

School vending documents

The amount of detail that the auditors review depends on the type of vending in your school. (See Chapter 20: Vending Services.)

- An audit of full-service vending includes a review of the vending contract to ensure that purchasing procedures were followed (e.g., bid, price quote), a review of the commission agreement to ensure that commissions were received at the intervals listed in the contract, and that the school's profit is reasonable. Auditors also verify that funds were receipted and deposited appropriately. If needed, they may gather information from the vending company to compare to the school's records.

- An audit of school-operated vending includes a review of inventory storage, access to vending machine keys, controls over money collected (e.g., receipts and deposits), disbursements to companies (e.g., purchasing guidelines were followed), and a count of current vending stock. The auditors use this information to calculate the expected ending inventory, as compared to the stock on hand.

- When a school uses a combination of full-service vending and school-operated vending, auditors may investigate any of the preceding areas.

Working and Communicating with the Audit Team

Most internal and external auditors conduct an entrance interview and an exit conference with you to introduce and close the audit. These are important opportunities for you to ask questions and clarify your concerns. Take advantage of this time.

- During the entrance interview, you should introduce the staff member you want the auditors to work with during the audit. This is also the opportunity for you and the audit team to discuss what areas are to be reviewed and the audit team's expectations. Be sure to ask (if you do not know) what physical space the auditors need while in your school (e.g., a conference room with phone, copier), the estimated time the auditors expect to be at your location, and other questions that may assist your staff in preparing for the audit.

- At the exit conference, the auditors discuss with you their findings and recommendations. It is important to note that most school activity funds are on a cash basis of accounting, wherein money is recorded in the bookkeeping system when it is received and spent. This method is not in conformity with generally accepted accounting principles. If this is the case with your school, the audit may include a clarifying statement saying that the school's bookkeeping system is not in conformity with generally accepted accounting

If you have any concerns about your bookkeeper's accuracy or honesty, choose someone other than your bookkeeper to work with the auditors.

principles. This does not mean there is a problem at your school. It is a way to inform interested parties that the school does not use the "accrual method" of accounting, in which expenditures are posted in the bookkeeping system when the merchandise or service is received and not when the invoice is paid (Fisher, Taylor, & Leer, 1982).

- The exit conference is also a good time to ask for any audit comments in writing, if you have concerns or questions that you need to direct to the district office. If you disagree with the findings and recommendations, call the central office for guidance while the auditors are present.

- Remember that auditors are more than just "financial watchdogs." Over the past few years, the role of internal auditors has changed, now allowing them to offer advice to improve the general operation of an organization (Sweeney, 2002). A well-trained auditor has experience in data collection and financial management software, and a good understanding of the school environment. Tap into auditors' professional training and experience by asking them to suggest improvements that will allow you more time to focus on instruction in your school.

Summary

Audits tend to be stressful for you and your office staff, particularly if audits are an integral part of your evaluation as a principal. Bookkeepers feel the stress most because they know that you rely heavily on them. If you use the guidelines in this chapter—and in each chapter of this book—to increase your working knowledge of money management at the school level, over time, your audits will go smoothly.

19

Transfers and Adjustments

Transfers and Adjustments— *Authorized changes in the bookkeeping of school accounts. Adjustments are bookkeeping transactions used to correct human errors. Transfers are bookkeeping transactions to move funds from one account to another.*

On occasion, it is necessary to alter bookkeeping entries for school activity funds to correct accounting errors or (when allowable by district guidelines) to move money from one account to another. Transfers and adjustments are similar, in that they both move funds between accounts within the bookkeeping system. However, there is a big difference in *when* you use each:

- An *adjustment* takes place to correct a previous posting (i.e., correct an error).
- A *transfer* takes place any time you need to move a portion or all of the balance of one account to another account. For example, at the end of a student fund-raising event, you might need to move the profit from the specific fund-raising account to the account where the money will be spent. In another situation, you may need to transfer money from one account to another to cover unexpected expenses.

Figure 19.1 provides a comparison of the characteristics of both transfers and adjustments.

For another example of transfers and adjustments, think of your personal bank accounts. If the bank mistakenly charges your account for a check written against another account, the bank would perform an adjustment to correct the error. If you want to move money from your savings account to your checking account, you would ask the bank to transfer the money or execute the transfer yourself electronically.

It is important to note that transfers and adjustments that occur without the permission of school administration could be a means of concealing theft of school funds. This chapter provides the guidelines you'll need to ensure the successful completion of authorized adjustments and transfers.

FIGURE **19.1**

Features of Transfers and Adjustments

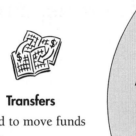

Transfers
• Used to move funds
• Necessary to close books
• Executed as needed

Documentation required
•
Approval required
•
Numbered and tracked
•
Net to zero

Adjustments
• Used to correct errors
• Executed when discovered

Procedures for Making Adjustments and Transfers

Transfers and adjustments should be monitored by you, the principal, and they should always be accompanied by clear documentation authorizing the change (Virginia Department of Education, 1989). Form 19-A and Form 19-B are completed examples of adjustment and transfer forms that include all the necessary documentation required for a principal's written approval. Remember that the role of the bookkeeper is to *process* a transfer or an adjustment, not to *authorize* it.

Adjustment Form
(see Appendix B, p. 142)

Transfer Form
(see Appendix B, p. 142)

• As the principal, you can give your written approval before or after the bookkeeper posts a change to the bookkeeping records. There are advantages and disadvantages to each option.

– Prior approval means you must approve the transaction *before* the bookkeeper enters it into the system. This practice reinforces the principle that the bookkeeper *never* makes changes without administrative authorization. Note, though, that prior approval does not prevent the bookkeeper from making an entry that is different from the one you approved.

- Giving your approval *after* the bookkeeper has made the entry allows you to see what the bookkeeper actually entered into the system. If the entry is not what you approved, the transaction can be corrected with an additional adjustment entry. The drawback is the risk that a bookkeeper could make a change and fail to obtain a verifying signature. The busier the school, the greater the chance this will occur.

- Some computerized bookkeeping systems allow the bookkeeper to enter a transaction and to print an approval voucher, meaning you can review the entry before the bookkeeper actually posts it. This is the preferred method; if it is available to you, use it.

- All requests for the transfer of funds should be authorized in writing and given to the bookkeeper to process. The approving requestor can be either the principal or a sponsor, but never the bookkeeper. For example, the teacher in charge of the staff remembrance fund may request a transfer from the staff vending machine account to the "Sunshine Fund" for a faculty gift. Insist that the request be in writing and attach it to the transfer form.

- *Never* authorize an adjustment or a transfer without backup documentation. If the bookkeeper has prepared an adjustment to correct a previous error, require the bookkeeper to attach the original transaction record so that you can see that the error did occur and that the entry is truly a correction. Remember, a transfer must originate from someone other than the bookkeeper.

- Each adjustment and transfer should be numbered and tracked. Most, if not all, computerized bookkeeping programs number these transactions and track them for you in printable reports. Such tracking is a big help in the monitoring process.

Accounting Rules for Transfers and Adjustments

- Transfers can only be made between the same type of account. In other words, transfers are only allowable from a bank account to a bank account (e.g., from the checking account to the savings account) or from one activity fund account to another (e.g., from the general fund to the honor society fund).

- Adjustments can be from any type of account to any other type of account, because the action is taken to correct an error.

- Both transfers and adjustments must net to zero. In other words, the increase amount must be equal to the decrease amount (e.g., transfer of $50 from staff vending to staff remembrance). See the examples provided in Forms 19-A and 19-B.

Frequency of Transfers and Adjustments

- Adjustments to the bookkeeping system should be made as soon as an error is discovered.

- Transfers can be limited to a particular time period (e.g., once a month, once a week), or they can take place at any time during the school year. Keep in mind that the greater the number of transfers within an account, the more complex—and difficult to analyze—that account's financial history becomes.

- Transfers are usually necessary at the end of every school year to close the school's books from one fiscal year (July 1 to June 30) to the next (e.g., you'll need to transfer profit from the school picture fund-raising account to the activity fund accounts where you plan to spend the profit). Some school districts prohibit transfers between accounts funded from the district's operating budget (e.g., instructional supplies and office equipment). Ask your district accounting or budget departments for written guidelines and follow these guidelines to the letter.

- If you are a new principal, you may want to hold your approval of both transfers and adjustments for several months until you are comfortable with the school's finances. Paper documents can be used to track needed adjustments and requested transfers until you know the staff, your financial responsibilities, and the bookkeeping account structure. It is better to delay your approval of transfers and adjustments for a time than to sign several in error. Changes can be reversed, of course, but you may be unknowingly creating deficit accounts because of upcoming expenses or assisting a bookkeeper in covering up unauthorized use of funds.

Optional Transfers for the Experienced Principal

Prior to the start of the school year, you may want to transfer a certain amount from your general fund to cover the anticipated monthly obligations to be paid from this account (e.g., small maintenance items, school cell phones, and copier supplies). By making transfers "early," based on the past spending history of an account, you can minimize or eliminate the need to use transfers during the year to prevent accounts from going in the red. A well-prepared budget, based on the history of past expenditures, can help reduce the need for these kinds of transfers. For more information on the budgeting process and estimating revenue and expenditures, see Chapter 15: The School Budget.

Summary

Transfers and adjustments are always necessary at certain times during the school year to correct accounting errors and to move funds from one account to another. Follow the guidelines in this chapter to ensure that adjustments to accounts and transfers between accounts are made with your knowledge and written approval—and not simply at the suggestion of your bookkeeper. Remember that you and your bookkeeper are a team, but you, as the principal, are ultimately responsible for the integrity of the school's bookkeeping system.

20

Vending Services

School Vending—*A type of ongoing fund raising reliant on the sale of drinks and snacks from a machine. The profits from sales benefit either the students or staff, depending on where the machines are located and who purchases the items (e.g., machines in a student hallway collect student funds, machines in the teachers' lounge collect staff funds).*

Vending services in schools can be a substantial source of revenue, depending on the number of machines, types of snacks, and the age of students (Hardy, 1999). But if vending machines are not monitored carefully, they can also be revenue drains, due to loss or theft. Stock for the machines may be damaged from careless or prolonged storage. Staff members in charge may give stock away or "borrow" from the vending machine proceeds. In addition, administrative time spent correcting these kinds of problems takes away from the more important aspects of the principalship. Follow the guidelines in this chapter to prevent embarrassing situations that could lead to repayment costs or staff dismissal.

Vending Service Options

- As principal, you can choose from three options for handling vending services, provided, of course, that your district allows each school the autonomy of selecting a type of service. With each option, the school's responsibility and potential for profits vary.

  – *Full-service vending:* The vending company oversees all aspects of vending service. The school receives a commission check, but the vending company provides the machines, stocks the machines, oversees machine maintenance (which includes refunding money lost in malfunctioning machines), and collects and counts the money from the machines. The school's time commitment and bookkeeping responsibilities are limited.

– *School-operated vending.* In this arrangement, the school purchases or rents vending machines, orders and stocks merchandise, and collects the money. In the long run, school-operated vending provides an opportunity for more profit, but also increases the potential for loss or theft.

– *Shared vending.* The school and the vending company share responsibility for the operation of the vending service. For example, the vending company might stock the machines, and the school might pay the vending company for the products and collect the money from the machines. This arrangement affords a higher potential for profit than full-service vending, but it does require increased staff and bookkeeping time and has a higher potential for theft.

• In evaluating your current or future vending services, be sure to consider the key advantages and disadvantages of each option (see Figure 20.1). Weigh the required staff time commitment and the risk factors before you decide in favor of higher profits.

FIGURE 20.1

Comparison of Vending Service Options

Factor	Full-Service Vending	School-Operated Vending	Shared Vending
Profit potential	low	high	medium
Staff time investment (handling cash/inventory)	low	high	medium
Risk of staff/student theft	low	high	medium
School responsible for inventory storage and security?	no	yes	no
School responsible for machine malfunction?	no	yes	no

tip

Consider full-service vending at a lower profit, and reduce the risk of internal theft.

Purchasing Procedures for Vending Services

• Before your school arranges for vending services, consider entering into a cooperative contract among schools or for the district as a whole, which is likely to increase your school's profit percentage. School vending is big business for vendors, who benefit from sales and build product recognition among students and staff (Zorn, 1999). Vendors are willing to make profit and service concessions for a large share of the school district's vending contract.

• If your school decides to make an independent vending arrangement, be sure to confirm the appropriate purchasing method to ensure compliance with state purchasing laws and district procedures. Find out the answers to these questions:

– Is a formal bid required?

– Is a price quote required?

– Is a purchase order or written contract sufficient?

Selecting the Best Vendor

Once you have decided the type of service to be offered and the appropriate purchasing procedure, the next step is to select a reliable, reputable vendor. Here are our suggested guidelines for evaluating prospective vendors. (See Figure 20.2 for a graphic summary.)

- Review the vendor's past performance (e.g., does the vendor have a track record of offering satisfactory service to other schools?).

- Confirm the percentage of profit offered by the vendor (e.g., the company offers 40 percent of gross sales).

- Assess what service the vendor will provide (e.g., restocking schedule, routine maintenance).

- Confirm the procedure for returned or refused items (i.e., will the company accept these items, or is the school required to purchase the items out of its profit?).

- Compare the retail price range of the inventory items (i.e., are the items within a price range consistent with the purchasing power of the students and staff?)

- Confirm the items to be sold (e.g., are fruit drinks and water sold or just sodas?) When you are deciding what items your school's vending machines will stock, remember that students are a captive audience and their health should be a primary consideration (Sheehan, 1999).

Make sure the percentage of profit is reasonable for the administrative effort required.

▌ FIGURE **20.2**

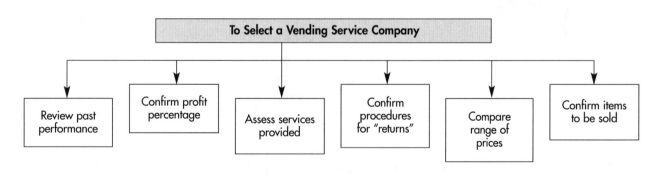

Responsibilities for Vending Services

In this section, we describe the typical staff responsibilities related to vending services, depending upon the vending service arrangement (school-operated or full-service). Shared vending between the school and vending company is not addressed here because responsibilities can vary within these arrangements. However, if your staff members are stocking items or collecting cash from machines, pay close attention to the advice in the section on school-operating vending services.

FORM 20-A

Vending Service
Authorization and
Financial Report
(see Appendix B, p. 143)

Stay within your school district's limit for holding money overnight.

➤ **School-Operated Vending Services: The Principal's Duties**

- Review state and federal regulations and school board policies that pertain to the allowable hours of vending operation and the location of vending machines. Restrict the hours of student access to vending services accordingly (e.g., prohibit vending machine use between 11:00 a.m. and 2:00 p.m.).

- Choose items to be stocked and sold (e.g., a balance of nutritious items and non-nutritious items).

- Designate two staff members (other than your bookkeeper) to serve as sponsors and oversee vending service. Placing two people in charge will reduce the risk of error and theft. Meet with the sponsors to review their key responsibilities, including the submission of fund-raising permits, collection and receipting duties, and inventory security.

- Give the vending machine keys to someone other than the two sponsors (e.g., an assistant principal). This precaution is an important internal control to protect machine stock and funds.

- Prohibit students from assisting sponsors with collecting duties.

➤ **School-Operated Vending Services: The Sponsors' Duties**

Remember, vending services are a type of fund-raising activity, just like a candy sale or the sale of school bumper stickers. Therefore, sponsors are responsible for obtaining administrative authorization, maintaining a clear audit trail, and securing inventory and funds throughout the course of the "event" (typically, the entire school year).

Duties at the beginning of the school year (prior to service).

- Complete a fund-raising permit (see Form 20-A) for each vending machine and submit the forms to the principal for approval.

- Review district policy regarding the receipt and deposit of funds collected. If there are restrictions on the amount of money that your school can hold in the building overnight, sponsors may need to collect and deposit vending machine funds daily. If not, and if volume of usage is low, money should be collected, counted, and deposited weekly.

Duties during the school year

- Monitor inventory levels closely and place orders to replenish stock in a timely manner to avoid major complaints from users and reduced profits from idle machines.

- Verify inventory quality and quantity each time a delivery is made.

- Secure the inventory items to prevent loss or damage (e.g., lock the storage area; restrict key access; ensure rodents and other pests do not have easy access; protect items from water damage).

- Collect funds from the machine according to the agreed-upon schedule. Sponsors should collect and count the money and unsold stock as a two-person team, and then turn the money in to the bookkeeper, along with a vending receipt (see Form 20-B) and written documentation reconciling items sold with funds collected.

- Secure the funds collected at the end of the day (e.g., forward the money to the bookkeeper for deposit; make a night deposit, if necessary).

- Set up a reimbursement procedure for vending customers. Customers who lose money in a vending machine should go to the main office and fill out a reimbursement voucher. After the bookkeeper obtains an authorizing signature, the customer can be reimbursed the next day. (For related information, see Chapter 13: The Petty Cash Fund.)

Duties at the end of the school year

- Count the entire inventory both in machines and in storage.

- Return unsold inventory to the vendor for the summer, if possible.

- Prepare any internal documents required by the school division (e.g., a fund-raiser financial report; see Form 20-A).

- Verify that the school received the appropriate percentage of profit based on the agreement between the school and the vendor (e.g., if the money the school is to receive is 40 percent of the sales, multiple the total sales by .40).

- Discuss the success of vending with the principal (i.e., was it profitable? beneficial to students and staff?).

➤ Full-Service Vending: The Principal's Duties

Although there is less staff involvement in full-service vending because the vending company handles most of the responsibilities, the principal must still perform an important monitoring function to ensure a profitable vending operation.

Duties at the beginning of the school year (prior to service)

- Obtain a competitive commission rate by comparing vending services. Check with your district purchasing department if you need assistance.

- Confirm the vendor's cash receipts procedures. Today, most large vending machines have internal counting mechanisms that tally the number of items sold to ensure the accuracy of commission payments. However, if you are using a small vending company, which may not have the latest machines or proper controls, it's best to have a staff member join the vendor's representative in counting cash removed from a machine. Both should sign off on the cash counted, and the school should retain a copy of the count.

- Ensure that commission checks are received at the appropriate times and deposited in the school's checking account in a timely manner. Monitor the amount of your commission at least twice a year for reasonableness.

Duties at the end of the school year

- Review the success of the vending service with the appropriate staff.

- Make notes for the future on ways to improve vending services (e.g., limit the amount of inventory or type of snacks and drinks to be sold).

- Contact the vending company to discuss any concerns, such as poor machine maintenance, damaged items for sale, or low profit margin.

FORM **20-B**

Individual Receipt
(Vending Services)
(see Appendix B, p. 143)

tip

Always track inventory and sales to verify your profit percentage.

Summary

Vending services provide a convenience to staff and students and a ready means of potentially substantial profit, depending on the size of your school and the age of your students. Planning with responsible staff members and the vendor will help ensure a successful operation.

Unfortunately, if staff members do not carefully follow the procedures outlined above, school vending also provides an opportunity for the loss of products and theft of funds. Because the principal is ultimately accountable for the loss of school funds, it is your responsibility to understand the risks inherent in school vending and implement the appropriate procedural remedies so that school vending is a good experience for everyone.

Appendix A

Financial Checklist for Principals

As a principal, you have many important responsibilities within the bookkeeping function. This checklist provides a list of the key financial activities—annual, quarterly, monthly, and weekly—for you to coordinate with your planning calendar throughout the year. It also includes references to chapters that you may find helpful as sources of further information.

Annual Periodic Financial Tasks

➤ New Spending Year: July

Meet with your bookkeeper to review her role and responsibilities. Ask the following questions to obtain an idea of your school's business practices during the past year:

❑ Are our bank accounts earning interest at a competitive rate?

❑ Do we have obsolete checks or receipt books in our school? If not, when were they destroyed or returned to the central office? (See Chapter 6: Employee Embezzlement.)

❑ Where is our inventory log of teacher receipt books?

❑ How often do you review teacher receipt books to ensure that receipts are issued in numerical order and that all three copies of voided receipts are intact?

❑ Have individual receipts been issued to students and parents when the amount collected exceeds $3?

❑ Are purchase orders prepared so that they are specific as to quantity, price, and delivery instructions before my signature is requested?

❑ Prepare purchase orders for the new school year (e.g., copy machine paper, school store supplies).

❏ Do "blanket purchase orders" for general items, such as office supplies, include a "not-to-exceed amount"?

❏ How often do you review open (i.e., unfilled) purchase orders?

❏ How often is our school's financial statement reconciled with statements from the bank for checking and saving accounts? (See Chapter 3: Bank Reconciliation.)

❏ Do you ever sign my name in my absence?

❏ Are all payments to school employees for services rendered (e.g., security officers, concession workers) processed through our district payroll office?

❏ How often do you reconcile the petty cash fund? (See Chapter 13: The Petty Cash Fund.)

❏ Are financial reports completed for events involving ticket sales? Is the number of the last ticket sold included? Where is our ticket inventory stored and who has a key? (See Chapter 2: Admission Tickets.)

❏ Are all fund-raising permits signed before a fund-raising campaign begins? Is the unsold inventory stored in a secure location? Who has a key? (See Chapter 9: Fund-Raising Events.)

❏ Who has keys to our drink and snack machines? Do we have excess inventory under lock and key? Who has access? (See Chapter 20: Vending Services.)

❏ Are you aware that I rely on you to keep me informed regarding money matters?

Complete the following tasks with *knowledgeable staff* (e.g., department heads):

❏ Review your school's budget for the upcoming year. Allow 2–3 days to establish expenditure and revenue targets for each account with your bookkeeper and other knowledgeable staff members. (See Chapter 15: The School Budget.)

❏ Enter funds in the appropriate accounts to reflect your projected budget.

❏ Finalize your purchase orders for fall supplies so that they are received prior to the teachers' return. Encumber funds that are obligated by purchase orders. (See Chapter 7: Encumbrance of Funds.)

❏ Open a purchase order in the name of each teacher in the amount of the central office's or PTA's supply allocation per teacher. (See Chapter 17: Staff Reimbursement.)

❏ Ensure that you, your bookkeeper, and all check signers are bonded financially.

❏ Review financial problems and successes from the prior school year (e.g., fund-raising events, purchase orders, credit/purchasing cards, and field trips).

❏ Review the latest audit findings and recommendations to establish corrective measures for the current school year. (See Chapter 18: Surviving an Audit.)

❏ Meet with the assistant principal who will act as financial administrator in your absence. Define dollar limits and the types of expenditures that can be approved in your absence. Advise your bookkeeper of these decisions.

❏ Take a well-deserved vacation!

Complete the following tasks with *appropriate staff* (e.g., club sponsors, school store sponsors, vending services sponsors):

❑ Meet with appropriate staff members regarding the sale of admission tickets for athletic events, performances, school fairs, and the like. Discuss inventory of tickets, payment of event workers, and profit. (See Chapter 2: Admission Tickets.)

❑ Review your vending machine contracts with appropriate staff and review your profit from the past year. (See Chapter 20: Vending Services.)

❑ Plan for the operation of your school store. Determine which staff members will operate the store, maintain the inventory records, and stock items. Update your written procedures. Advise your bookkeeper. (See Chapter 16: The School Store.)

❑ Make sure your staff handbook is updated on financial topics (e.g., turning collected money into the office, issuing of receipts, purchase orders, purchasing cards). Advise your bookkeeper of changes. (See Chapter 1: Activity Fund Safeguards.)

➤ **Arrival of Teachers: August**

❑ Hold a staff meeting to review the financial portion of the staff handbook. Discuss new procedures or troubling issues (e.g., holding of collected money overnight, petty cash fund). Have your bookkeeper in attendance.

❑ Ensure that staff members begin the school year aware of the fiscal responsibilities that go with handling and spending school money. Give them an opportunity to ask questions.

❑ Meet with the staff remembrance committee to review how funds will be collected and allocated to honor life events such as births and weddings. (See Chapter 10: Gifts to Students or Staff.)

➤ **Quarterly Tasks: September 30, January 30, March 30**

❑ If expenditures and fund-raising activities have been extensive, meet with your bookkeeper to revisit expenditure and revenue targets for each account in order to revise your original budget plan. (See Chapter 15: The School Budget.)

❑ Review financial problems or concerns (e.g., negative balance in accounts) with your bookkeeper and make appropriate transfers and adjustments before the school year ends. (See Chapter 19: Transfers and Adjustments.)

❑ Review the bank reconciliation for checking and savings accounts; make sure that your account does not exceed the allowable amount insured by the Federal Deposit Insurance Corporation (FDIC).

❑ Review district deadlines (usually early spring) for spending funds allocated from the central office. *Always* spend district money allocated to your school (e.g., office supply allocation) before spending school funds (e.g., general fund), which can be rolled over to the next year.

❑ Review vending service commissions.

➤ **End of the School Year: June 15–June 30**

❑ Review the year-end adjustments and transfers. (See Chapter 4: Bookkeeping Basics.)

❑ Follow-up on unfilled purchase orders and cancel those that are not needed.

❑ Prepare for the end-of-the-year audit. (See Chapter 18: Surviving an Audit.)

❑ Ask two staff members to conduct an inventory of all supplies remaining in your school store. Review the results before processing purchase orders for additional supplies. (See Chapter 16: The School Store.)

Monthly Tasks

❑ Review the monthly bank statement and bank reconciliation.

❑ Compare the monthly financial reports generated by your bookkeeper with the reconciliation of the bank statement.

❑ Discuss any financial or procedural concerns that your bookkeeper may have (e.g., Mrs. Jones holds money overnight, incomplete fund-raising statements, vendors who have not billed).

❑ Review items approved in your absence (e.g., purchase orders, checks, purchasing card statements).

❑ Discuss your bookkeeper's review of the following:
   ❑ Open purchase orders
   ❑ Financial statements for fund-raising events
   ❑ Financial statements for field trips
   ❑ Financial statements for athletic or other admission-ticket events
   ❑ Account balances (e.g., no account has an unexpected negative balance)

Weekly Tasks

Review documentation that requires your approval:

❑ Purchase orders

❑ Checks

❑ Field trip authorizations and financial statements (See Chapter 8: Field Trips.)

❑ Fund-raising event authorizations and financial reports (See Chapter 9: Fund-Raising Events.)

❑ Transfers (See Chapter 19: Transfers and Adjustments.)

❑ Adjustments

❑ Electronic banking transfers (See Chapter 11: Online Purchasing and Electronic Banking Transfers.)

Ask your bookkeeper these questions:

❑ Are there any sponsors/teachers who are not following the receipting or purchase order procedures (e.g., holding funds, purchasing before receiving written approval)?

❑ Are there any problems with vendors (e.g., vendors stating items have been received but teachers failing to notify the bookkeeper that the items have arrived)?

❑ Are all financial reports, including the bank reconciliation, up to date?

❑ Are checks and purchase orders waiting to be signed?

❑ Are the bank deposits being made daily? If not, how much is being kept in the building, and where is it being stored? How are funds secured?

❑ Is the librarian maintaining a list of collected fines by date and student? Are fines and the list sent to the office weekly?

❑ Are school store receipts sent to the office daily?

❑ Are teacher receipts issued in numerical order? Are all three copies of voided receipts left in receipt books?

❑ Is all documentation (e.g., vendor's invoice, packing slip) attached when checks are prepared for my signature?

❑ Are all checks, including voided checks, accounted for?

❑ Are deposit slips on file for audit review?

❑ Are all payments to school employees for services rendered (e.g., ticket sales, concession workers) processed through our district payroll office?

❑ Are there any pending items that we need to discuss (e.g., outstanding financial report for a field trip completed more than a month ago)?

❑ Do you have any special bookkeeping concerns or suggestions for improvements?

Appendix B

Financial Forms

This section presents 26 sample financial forms to illustrate some of the book-keeping procedures and safeguards described in the chapter text.

List of Forms

Paradise School **Ticket Sales Report**						
Type of Event	*Varsity Football Game*					
Date	*October 31, 2003*					
Ticket Color	**Type of Admission**	**(a)** **Beginning Ticket Number**	**(b)** **Ending Ticket Number + 1**	**# Tickets Sold** **(b - a)**	**Ticket Price**	**Total Received**
Blue	*Adult*	*505*	*845*	*340*	*$5.00*	*$1,700.00*
Green	*Student*	*2000*	*2400*	*400*	*$3.00*	*$1,200.00*
Red	*Child*	*175*	*185*	*10*	*$2.00*	*$20.00*
					Total Receipts	**$2,920.00**
					Change Fund	*$500.00*
				Total Money (Total Receipts + Change Fund)		**$3,420.00**
				Actual Amount in Cash Box/Drawer		*$3,418.00*
				Over/short		*($2.00)*
James F. Ruppe			*October 31, 2003*			
Ticket Seller's Signature			**Date Submitted**			
Patrick Lee			*October 31, 2003*			
Event Coordinator's Signature			**Date Approved**			

FORM 2-A

Ticket Sales Report

This form is used to track ticket sales for sporting events, dances, and other school functions.

Paradise School **Event Financial Report**			
Type of Event	*Varsity Football Game*		
Date	*October 31, 2003*		
Receipts			
Ticket Sales Report	*J. Ruppe*	*$2,920.00*	
Ticket Sales Report	*R. Cash*	*$1,500.00*	
Ticket Sales Report	*L. Shambra*	*$1,580.00*	
	Total Receipts		$6,000.00
Disbursements			
Security	*City police*	*$500.00*	
Event Workers	*Ticket takers/Ticket sellers*	*$200.00*	
Officiating	*Game officials*	*$300.00*	
Benefits Cost	*FICA payroll taxes*	*$53.55*	
	Total Payments		$1,053.55
	Profit From the Event		**$4,946.45**
	Profit Percentage		**82%**
Patrick Lee		*November 7, 2003*	
Event Coordinator's Signature		**Date Prepared**	
Noah Daniel		*November 7, 2003*	
Student Activities Coordinator's Signature		**Date Approved**	

FORM 2-B

Event Financial Report

This form is used to report financial information after a ticket sales event. Note that event disbursements should include FICA payroll tax on wages paid to "employees" working the event. In this example, FICA is calculated at .0765 of wages paid to security personnel and ticket sellers/ticket takers; game officials are contracted service providers.

FORM **3-A**

Bank Reconciliation
Form

This form is used to reconcile the bank statement balance with the bookkeeping balance. It is designed for the principal's approval. If the bank reconciliation is prepared correctly, the "Adjusted Bank Statement Balance" (Part 1, item 3) and the "Adjusted Bookkeeping Balance" (Part 2, item 7) will match, and the "Out-of-Balance Amount" will be zero.

Paradise School
Bank Reconciliation Form

Part 1: Bank Statement Balance

		Date			Amount
Balance per the Bank Statement		*10/31/03*			***$10,985.00***
1.	**Deposits in Transit**	Date		Amount	
		10/31/03		*$1,500.00*	
		10/31/03		*$6,000.00*	
			Total		$7,500.00
2.	**Outstanding Checks**		Check #	Amount	
			1501	*($84.00)*	
			1502	*($358.00)*	
			1503	*($35.00)*	
			Total		($477.00)
3.	**Adjusted Bank Statement Balance**				**$18,008.00**

Part 2: School's Bookkeeping Balance

		Date			Amount
Balance per School Bookkeeping Records		*10/31/03*			***$18,213.00***
4.	**Interest Earned**				*$20.00*
5.	**Non-Sufficient Funds (NSF) Fees**			Amount	
	Joe Smith Check			*($200.00)*	
			Total		($200.00)
6.	**Bank Charges (Service and Miscellaneous)**			Amount	
	Printing deposit slips			*($25.00)*	
			Total		($25.00)
7.	**Adjusted Bookkeeping Balance**				**$18,008.00**
8.	**Out-of-Balance Amount**				**$0.00**

Doris Ruppe	*November 12, 2003*
Preparer's Signature	**Date Prepared**
Angela Poirson	*November 13, 2003*
Principal's Signature	**Date Approved**

Paradise School
Purchase Order

School Street Address	777 Eden Way
City, State, ZIP Code	Garden City, VA 23377
Phone #	757-555-0322
Fax #	757-555-4321
School's Tax Exempt #	57-003321

Ship to address above

Vendor Name	Office Wholesale Discounters
Vendor Address	532 6th Street
Vendor City, State, ZIP	Garden City, VA 23377
Phone #	757-555-4980

PO # 55500	**Terms of Purchase**	PO Date September 10, 2003	
Quantity	Units	Item Description	Unit Cost	Total Cost

Quantity	Units	Item Description	Unit Cost	Total Cost
		Office Supplies	$100.00	

Restrictions: Use of vendor's purchasing card not to exceed $100 (September 10 to October 31, 2003)

		Total	$0.00

Betty Diamond, Principal's Secretary	*September 10, 2003*
Purchase Requestor's Signature	Date Requested
Angela Poirson	*September 12, 2003*
Principal's Signature	Date Approved

FORM 5-A

Blanket Purchase Order (Credit/Purchasing Card Use)

This prenumbered, multicopy form is used to record staff requests to purchase materials and supplies from outside vendors or, as in this example, to authorize a staff member's use of a vendor-dedicated school credit/purchasing card. At least one copy of the purchase order must remain with the bookkeeper.

Paradise School
Encumbrances

Account #	5605
Account Name	Honor Society—Fund Raising

Description	Purchase Order #	Purchase Order Amount (Encumbrance)	Invoice #	Invoice Amount (Adjustment)	Fund Balance
Beginning Balance					**$1,000.00**
1. *Inventory, Peanut Fund Raiser*	55561	$500.00			$500.00
Check #1450 for PO #55561			7501	$500.00	**$500.00**
2. *Student Prizes*	55591	$150.00			$350.00
Check #1451 for PO #55591			102303	$100.00	**$400.00**
3.					
4.					

FORM 7-A

Encumbrance Tracking Spreadsheet

This form is used to track open encumbrances (i.e., purchase orders that have not been paid).

This form is used to
record the principal's
approval of a field trip
and to report the trip's
financial information.

Paradise School
Field Trip Authorization

Name of the Field Trip	*Visit to The Jamestown Museum*
Date to Begin Collections	*October 17, 2003*
Date of the Field Trip	*October 31, 2003*
Teacher/Sponsor's Name	*Ryan Lee*
Group to Attend	*Honor Society*
Educational Benefits	*Correlates to Standards of Learning*
Principal's Signature	*Angela Poirson*
Date Approved	*9/3/03*

Field Trip Financial Report

Receipts	*See bookkeeper receipts #61, #62, #63 ($40)* *Transfer #5 ($400 profit from Peanut Sale)*	*$440.00*
Disbursements	*Check #1501 (museum fee), Check #1502 (bus service)*	*$442.00*
	Balance	**($2.00)**
Notes	*There was one indigent student. The PTA is to reimburse the school for student's trip fee.*	

Ryan Lee	*November 5, 2003*
Teacher/Sponsor's Signature	**Date Submitted**
Noah Daniel	*November 6, 2003*
Student Activities Coordinator's Signature	**Date Approved**

Paradise School **Individual Receipt**			
Student/Parent/Staff Receipt #	*00000541*		
Name of Payee	*Luis Hernandez*		
Date Received	*October 25, 2003*		
Payment Reason	**Description**	**Check Amount**	**Cash Amount**
Fund-Raising Event			
Field Trip	*Jamestown*		*$2.00*
Dues	*History Club*		*$5.00*
Textbook Fees	*Lost textbook*	*$35.00*	
Gym Suits			
Locks			
Other Fees			
	Subtotals	$35.00	$7.00
	Total		**$42.00**
Ryan Lee	*October 25, 2003*		
Teacher/Sponsor's Signature	**Date Issued**		

FORM **8-B**

Individual Receipt
(Field Trip)

This prenumbered, multicopy form is used to receipt money collected from a student, parent, or staff member for a variety of purposes. In this example, the Honor Society field trip sponsor (teacher Ryan Lee) has issued a receipt for field trip money collected from a student in his class, Honor Society member Luis Hernandez. Mr. Lee also collected funds for other purposes from Luis on the same day. The money is recorded as either cash or check, and the purpose is indicated. One copy of the completed receipt form goes to the payee (Luis), one copy is submitted to the bookkeeper with the collected funds, and one copy remains in Mr. Lee's individual receipt book.

FORM **8-C**

Group Receipt (Field Trip)

This prenumbered, multi-copy form is used to receipt small amounts of money collected from students, parents, and staff for a common purpose. In this example, the field trip sponsor (Mr. Lee) has issued one group receipt for all field trip money collected on October 20. The money collected is recorded as either cash or check and the purpose of the collection is indicated. One copy of the completed receipt form is submitted to the bookkeeper with the collected funds and one copy remains in Mr. Lee's group receipt book.

Paradise School
Group Receipt

Group Receipt #	*0000073*		
Description	*Field Trip Fees—Jamestown Trip*		

Payees	Check Amount	Cash Amount
Ric Poirson	$2.00	
Noah Poirson	$2.00	
David Lynne		$2.00
John David	$2.00	
Subtotals	$6.00	$2.00
Total		**$8.00**

Ryan Lee	*October 20, 2003*
Teacher/Sponsor's Signature	**Date Issued**

FORM **8-D**

Field Trip Permission Form

This form is used to secure parental permission for students to attend field trips.

Paradise School
Parent/Guardian Field Trip Permission Form

Reason for Permission Request	*Field Trip to The Jamestown Museum*
Date of the Field Trip	*October 31, 2003*
Travel Provider	*Number One Bus Company*
Sponsor's Name	*Ryan Lee*
Sponsor's Phone #	*757-555-2222*
Group to Attend	*Honor Society*
Educational Benefits	*Correlates to Standards of Learning*
Principal's Signature	*Angela Poirson*
Date Approved	*9/3/03*

Parents/Guardians: **Please complete the section below and return.**

My child's name	
My name	
Emergency contact's name	
Emergency contact's phone #	
My child is covered by medical insurance.	Yes ☐ No ☐
	Name of policy:
If you approve your child's participation, please sign.	
	Signature (above) indicates child will attend field trip.
If you do not approve your child's participation, please sign.	Signature (below) indicates child will not attend field trip.
Date approved/not approved	

If you have questions regarding the field trip, call the sponsor listed at the top of the form.

FORM **8-E**

Field Trip Checklist

This form is used
to control field trip
information.

		Paradise School **Field Trip Checklist**			
Field Trip	*The Jamestown Museum*				
Field Trip Date	*October 31, 2003*				
Student	**Contact #**	**Permission**	**Paid**	**Parent Chaperone**	**Special Needs**
Noah Poirson	*555-1039*	*X*	*X*		
Ric Poirson	*555-1039*	*X*	*X*		
David Lynne	*555-7855*	*X*	*X*		
John David	*555-8159*	*X*	*X*		*PTA paid*
Thomas Kenyon	*555-3569*	*X*	*X*		
Zack Rogers	*555-7865*	*X*	*X*	*Jennifer Rogers*	
Amanda Wagner	*555-3731*	*X*	*X*		
Matthew Nguyen	*555-6804*	*X*	*X*		
Paul Harper	*555-5550*	*X*	*X*	*Penny Harper*	
Candy Colanna	*555-1923*	*X*	*X*		
Angela Parker	*555-7756*	*X*	*X*		
Lizzy Rivera	*555-7920*	*X*	*X*		*diabetic*
Jessica Gilmore	*555-1322*	*X*	*X*		
Luis Hernandez	*555-9114*	*X*	*X*		
Shanita Dawkins	*555-4878*	*X*	*X*		
Kayla Peeler	*555-0764*	*X*	*X*		
Michael Murray	*555-2650*	*X*	*X*		
Chris Desalvo	*555-4644*	*X*	*X*		
		Total Students	**18**		
		Total Chaperones	**2**		

Notes

Arrival time is set for 10:15 a.m. Guide confirmed for the "Life at Jamestown" hands-on history program (will be waiting at main desk). Lunch at 12:30. Buses arrive for return trip at 2 p.m. All students to Loading Area B by 2:15.

FORM **9-A**

Fund-Raising Event
Authorization and
Financial Report

This form is used to record
the principal's approval of
a fund-raising event and to
report the event's financial
information.

Paradise School
Fund-Raising Event Authorization

Name of the Event/Activity	*Honor Society Peanut Sale*
Date to Begin	*September 15, 2003*
Date to End	*October 3, 2003*
Event Sponsor's Name	*Ryan Lee*
Group to Receive Profit	*Honor Society for field trip to Jamestown*
Vendor	*Yummy Nut Co.*
Contracted Profit Percentage	*40%*
Principal's Signature	*Angela Poirson*
Date Approved	*9/3/03*

Fund-Raising Event Financial Report

Receipts	*See bookkeeper receipts #45, #56, #57, #60*	*$1,000.00*
Disbursements	*Check #1450 (peanut vendor), Check #1451 (student incentive prizes)*	*$600.00*
	Profit	**$400.00**
	Profit Percentage	**40%**
Students with Outstanding Items/Funds	*None*	

Ryan Lee	*October 10, 2003*
Event Sponsor's Signature	**Date**
Noah Daniel	*October 10, 2003*
Student Activities Coordinator's Signature	**Date**

Paradise School
Individual Receipt

Student/Parent/Staff Receipt #	00000209		
Name of Payee	Johnny Parker		
Date Received	October 6, 2003		

Payment Reason	Description	Check Amount	Cash Amount
Fund-Raising Event	Honor Society Peanut Sale	$2.00	$2.00
Field Trip			
Dues			
Textbook Fees			
Gym Suits			
Locks			
Other Fees			
	Subtotals	$2.00	$2.00
	Total		**$4.00**

Ryan Lee	*October 6, 2003*
Teacher/Sponsor's Signature	**Date Issued**

FORM 9-B

Individual Receipt
(Fund-Raising)

This prenumbered, multicopy form is used to receipt money collected from a student, parent, or staff member for a variety of purposes. In this example, the fund-raising event's sponsor (teacher Ryan Lee) has issued a receipt for Peanut Sale money turned in by Johnny Parker. The money collected is recorded as either cash or check, and its purpose is indicated. One copy of the completed receipt form goes to the payee (Johnny), one copy is submitted to the bookkeeper with the collected funds, and one copy remains in Mr. Lee's individual receipt book.

Paradise School
Group Receipt

Group Receipt #	0000067		
Description	Honor Society Peanut Sale		

Payees		Check Amount	Cash Amount
Noah Poirson			$2.00
Ric Poirson		$2.00	
Shanita Dawkins			$2.00
David Lynne			$2.00
Johnny Parker			$2.00
	Subtotals	$2.00	$8.00
	Total Received		**$10.00**

Ryan Lee	*September 30, 2003*
Teacher/Sponsor's Signature	**Date Issued**

FORM 9-C

Group Receipt
(Fund-Raising)

This prenumbered, multi-copy form is used to receipt small amounts of money collected from students, parents, or for a common purpose. In this example, the fund-raising event's sponsor has issued a group receipt for all Peanut Sale money collected on September 30. The money collected is recorded as either cash or check and the purpose of the collection is indicated. One copy of the completed receipt form is submitted to the bookkeeper with the collected funds and one copy remains in Mr. Lee's group receipt book.

FORM **9-D**

Fund-Raising
Event Sponsor's
Distribution List

This form is used to keep
an accurate count of
fund-raising merchandise
distributed for sale. In
this example, the unit
price for peanuts is $1.

Paradise School		
Sponsor's Distribution List		
Name of the Event/Activity	*Honor Society Peanut Sale*	
Date to Begin	*September 15, 2003*	
Date to End	*October 3, 2003*	
Sponsor's Name	*Ryan Lee*	
Date	**Name**	**Quantity**
9/15/03	*Ric Poirson*	*24*
9/15/03	*Noah Poirson*	*24*
9/15/03	*David Lynne*	*24*
9/15/03	*Luis Hernandez*	*24*
9/15/03	*Jessica Gilmore*	*12*
9/15/03	*Amanda Wagner*	*12*
9/15/03	*Matthew Nguyen*	*12*
9/15/03	*Johnny Parker*	*24*
9/15/03	*Shanita Dawkins*	*24*
9/25/03	*Noah Poirson*	*12*
9/25/03	*Ric Poirson*	*12*
	Total Items Distributed	**204**

Items Returned

Date	**Name**	**Quantity**
10/2/03	*David Lynne*	*4*
	Total Items Sold	**200**

Individuals with Outstanding Items/Funds

Johnny Parker owed and paid $4. See teacher receipt #209, dated 10/6/03.

Paradise School
Petty Cash Reimbursement Voucher

Voucher #	*10*
Name of Requestor	*Betty Diamond*
Department/Club Affiliation	*Office Secretary (General Fund)*
Amount Requested	*$15.00*
Description of Expenditure	*Purchase extra paper for printing invitations to School Open House.*
Signature of Administrator (reimbursement approved)	*Angela Poirson*
Date Reimbursement Approved	*October 23, 2003*
Signature of Requestor (reimbursement received)	*Betty Diamond*
Date Reimbursement Received	*October 24, 2003*

FORM 13-A

Petty Cash Reimbursement Voucher

This form is used to request and authorize staff reimbursement for petty cash expenditures.

Paradise School
Petty Cash Reconciliation Form

Reconciliation Period	*October 20–31*
Date of the Report	*October 31, 2003*

	(a) Total Petty Cash Fund	**$250.00**

Part 1: Petty Cash on Hand

Dollars by Denomination	Count	Amount
$20 bills	5	$100.00
$10 bills	5	$50.00
$5 bills	6	$30.00
$1 bills	25	$25.00

Coins by Type	Count	Amount
quarters	32	$8.00
dimes	5	$0.50
nickels	10	$0.50
pennies	100	$1.00

	(b) Total Petty Cash Available	**$215.00**

Part 2: Current Period Completed Vouchers

Voucher #	Description	Amount
10	Open House Invitations	$15.00
11	Lock Repair	$20.00

(c) Total Vouchers Expenditures (reimbursed by check # below)	**$35.00**
Activity Fund Check # *1503*	

(b) Total Cash Available + (c) Total Voucher Expenditures	**$250.00**

Doris Ruppe	*October 31, 2003*
Preparer's Signature	**Date Prepared**
Angela Poirson	*October 31, 2003*
Principal's Signature	**Date Approved**

FORM 13-B

Petty Cash Reconciliation Form

This form is used to reconcile the petty cash fund. In this example, activity fund check #1503 has been issued payable to "Petty Cash" to reimburse the fund for the listed petty cash expenditures. If all petty cash has been accounted for correctly, the sum of the "Total Petty Cash Available" (b) plus the "Total Current Period Expenditures" (c) will equal the "Total Petty Cash Fund" (a).

FORM **14-A**

Raffle Ticket Sales Report

This form is used to track ticket sales for sporting events, dances, and other school functions. In this example, it is tracking raffle ticket sales.

Paradise School
Ticket Sales Report

Type of Event	*Student Government Raffle*					
Date	*October 16, 2003*					

Ticket Color	**Type of Admission**	**(a) Beginning Ticket Number**	**(b) Ending Ticket Number + 1**	**# Tickets Sold (b - a)**	**Ticket Price**	**Total Received**
Orange	*Raffle*	*1*	*521*	*520*	*$1.00*	*$520.00*

Total Receipts	**$520.00**
Change Fund	*$10.00*
Total Money (Total Receipts + Change Fund)	**$530.00**
Actual Amount in Cash Box/Drawer	*$530.00*
Over/short	**$0.00**

Laura Hamlin	*October 16, 2003*
Ticket Seller's Signature	**Date Prepared**
Wayne Robbins	*October 16, 2003*
Raffle Coordinator's Signature	**Data Approved**

FORM **14-B**

Raffle Financial Report

This form is used to report financial information after a raffle.

Paradise School
Event Financial Report

Type of Event	*Student Government Raffle*		
Date	*October 21, 2003*		

Receipts			
Ticket Sales Report	*L. Hamlin*	*$520.00*	
Ticket Sales Report	*J. David*	*$460.00*	
Ticket Sales Report	*G. Bright*	*$445.00*	
	Total Receipts		$1,425.00

Disbursements			
Prizes Purchased	*Television with VCR*	*$500.00*	
Prizes Purchased	*Portable television*	*$200.00*	
Cost of Tickets	*Ticket printing fee*	*$15.30*	
	Total Disbursements		$715.30
	Profit From the Event		**$709.70**
	Profit Percentage		**50%**

Wayne Robbins	*October 21, 2003*
Raffle Coordinator's Signature	**Date Prepared**
Noah Daniel	*October 22, 2003*
Student Activities Coordinator's Signature	**Date Approved**

Paradise School **School Store Inventory**				
Item Description	**Quantity on Hand**	**Unit**	**Unit Cost**	**Total Value**
pencils	*2.50*	*box*	*$5.00*	*$12.50*
erasers	*1.25*	*box*	*$3.00*	*$3.75*
mechanical pencils	*0.50*	*box*	*$6.00*	*$3.00*
notepads	*3.00*	*box*	*$4.00*	*$12.00*
notebook paper	*4.75*	*box*	*$5.00*	*$23.75*
gym suits (girls' shorts)	*20.00*	*box*	*$15.00*	*$300.00*
gym suits (girls' tops)	*5.00*	*box*	*$12.00*	*$60.00*
gym suits (boys' shorts)	*10.00*	*box*	*$15.00*	*$150.00*
gym suits (boys' tops)	*2.00*	*box*	*$7.50*	*$15.00*
Value of In-Stock Inventory				**$580.00**
Cleveland Parker	*September 9, 2003*			
Store Sponsor's Signature	**Date Completed**			
Betty Diamond	*September 9, 2003*			
Second Inventory Counter's Signature	**Date Completed**			

FORM 16-A

School Store Physical Inventory Report

This form is used to account for the number of items in inventory in the school store. Note that because individual items in the inventory usually have a low monetary value, it is possible to conduct the physical count in terms of the number of boxes and partial boxes.

Paradise School **Purchase Order**				
School Street Address	*777 Eden Way*			
City, State, ZIP Code	*Garden City, VA 23377*			
Phone Number	*757-555-0322*			
Fax Number	*757-555-4321*			
School's Tax Exempt #	*57-003321*			
Ship to address above				
Vendor Name	*Cleveland Parker, School Store Sponsor*			
Vendor Address				
Vendor City, State, ZIP				
Phone Number				
PO # *55591*	**Terms of Purchase**		**PO Date** *October 20, 2003*	
Quantity	**Units**	**Item Description**	**Unit Cost**	**Total Cost**
10	*packages*	*pens*	*$2.50*	*$25.00*
5	*boxes*	*mechanical pencils*	*$6.00*	*$30.00*
Restrictions	*Not to exceed $100.* *In-house purchase order. Do not mail.*			
			Total	**$55.00**
Cleveland Parker, Sponsor	*October 20, 2003*			
Purchase Requestor's Signature	**Date Requested**			
Angela Poirson	*October 24, 2003*			
Principal's Signature	**Date Approved**			

FORM 17-A

Purchase Order (Staff Reimbursement Use)

This prenumbered, multi-copy form is used to purchase materials and supplies from outside vendors and/or for staff reimbursement requests for school-related expenses. In this example, the school store sponsor will be picking up and paying for the supplies, and the purchase order will not be mailed. Upon his return to the school, he will attach the store receipt to his copy of the purchase order and submit it to the book-keeper, who will prepare a check for the sponsor. In this case, the vendor copy of the purchase is not mailed to the vendor.

FORM **17-B**

Travel Expense Form
(Part A)

This two-part form is used to authorize and record staff's travel-related expenses. The tracking number (67219992 in this example) provides an additional means of identifying the payee.

Paradise School
Travel Expense Form

Tracking #	67219992
Traveler's Name	Patrick Lee
Starting Travel Date	October 7, 2003
Ending Travel Date	October 9, 2003
Trip Destination	Athletic Conference in Williamsburg, VA
Trip Purpose	To learn new ways to track athletic event sales using computer-generated tickets
Estimated Cost	$600.00
Principal's Approval	*Angela Poirson*
Date Approved	10/1/03

Part A: Itemized Expenses to be reimbursed by the school.
Please attach all original receipts.

Expenses	Date 10/7/03	Date 10/8/03	Date 10/9/03	Date	Date	Total
Registration Fee	$295.00					$295.00
Lodging	$95.20	$95.20				$190.40
Breakfast						
Lunch						
Dinner	$25.00	$25.00				$50.00
Airline/Train/Bus Fare						
Personal Vehicle (see Part B)	$14.40		$14.40			$28.80
Parking Tolls	$5.00	$5.00				$10.00
Presentation Materials						
Miscellaneous						
Subtotal by Date	*$434.60*	*$125.20*	*$14.40*			
				Total Travel Expenses		**$574.20**
				Less the Amount of the Travel Advance		**$500.00**
				Net Amount Due Traveler (Due School)		**$74.20**

Patrick Lee	*October 14, 2003*
Traveler's Signature	**Date Submitted**
Angela Poirson	*October 16, 2003*
Principal's Signature (approving reimbursement)	**Date Approved**

Paradise School
Travel Expense Form

Part B: Personal Vehicle Mileage Log and Expense Worksheet				
Tracking #	67219992			
Name of Traveler	Patrick Lee			
Street Address	123 Main Street			
City, State, ZIP	Suffolk, VA 23439			
Starting Travel Date	October 7, 2003			
Ending Travel Date	October 9, 2003			

Date	From	To	# Miles	Miles x $0.36 (2003 IRS rate)
10/7/03	Suffolk, VA	Williamsburg, VA	40	$14.40
10/9/03	Williamsburg, VA	Suffolk, VA	40	$14.40
		Total Mileage	80.00	
		Total Personal Vehicle Expense		**$28.80**
				carry this amount to Part A

Patrick Lee
Traveler's Signature

October 14, 2003
Date Submitted

FORM 17-B

Travel Expense Form (Part B)

A traveler completes Part B of the form when he or she uses a personal vehicle to travel to and from the travel destination.

Paradise School
Travel Advance Form

Name of Traveler	Patrick Lee
Funds Requested	$500.00
Reason for Trip	Athletic Conference
Trip Destination	Williamsburg, VA
Starting Travel Date	October 7, 2003
Ending Travel Date	October 9, 2003
Expense Form Due	October 16, 2003

Angela Poirson
Principal's Signature

October 1, 2003
Date Approved

Your signature as the Traveler, below, indicates that you have received the approved advance funds, that you will reimburse the school for funds received that are not spent on school business, and that you will submit your final expense form by the due date indicated.

Patrick Lee
Traveler's Signature

October 6, 2003
Date Funds Received

FORM 17-C

Travel Advance Form

This form is used to authorize a travel advance, to document the traveler's receipt of the funds, and to record the traveler's agreement to the terms of use.

FORM **19-A**

Adjustment Form

This form is used to record adjustments that will be made to the bookkeeping system.

	Paradise School **Adjustment Form**		
Adjustment #	*00008*		
Description	*Correction of bookkeeper receipt #1201 (9/28/03) posted incorrectly to the Student Vending Account. The correction is to the Staff Vending Account.*		

Move from Account	Account #	Amount
Student Vending	*4603*	*($100.00)*
	Total	*($100.00)*

Move to Account	Account #	Amount
Staff Vending	*5603*	*$100.00*
	Total	*$100.00*

Angela Poirson	*November 12, 2003*
Principal's Signature	**Date Approved**
Doris Ruppe	*November 13, 2003*
Bookkeeper's Signature	**Date Posted**

FORM **19-B**

Transfer Form

This form is used to record transfers of funds from one account to another account.

	Paradise School **Transfer Form**		
Transfer #	*00005*		
Description	*Move the $400 Peanut Sale profit from the Honor Society Fund-Raising Account to the Honor Society Field Trip Account.*		

Transfer from Account	Account #	Amount
Honor Society—Fund-Raising	*5605*	*($400.00)*
	Total	*($400.00)*

Transfer to Account	Account #	Amount
Honor Society—Field Trip	*7605*	*$400.00*
	Total	*$400.00*

Ryan Lee	*October 16, 2003*
Requestor's Signature	**Date Requested**
Angela Poirson	*October 17, 2003*
Principal's Signature	**Date Approved**
Doris Ruppe	*October 17, 2003*
Bookkeeper's Signature	**Date Posted**

Paradise School
Fund-Raising Event Authorization

Group to Receive Profit	*Staff Remembrance Fund*
Vendor	*Fizzy Soft Drink Company*
Contracted Profit Percentage	*30%*
Principal's Signature	*Angela Poirson*
Date Approved	*9/3/03*

Fund-Raising Event Financial Report

Receipts	*See listing of vending receipts for 9/15/03 to 6/30/04.*	*$1,000.00*
Disbursements	*Checks #1408, #1701, #2010 (to vendor)*	*$700.00*
	Profit	**$300.00**
	Profit Percentage	**30%**

Bonnie Heywood	*June 30, 2004*
Event Sponsor's Signature	**Date Submitted**
Alice Claywell	*June 30, 2004*
Student Activities Coordinator's Signature	**Date Approved**

Paradise School
Individual Receipt

Student/Parent/Staff Receipt #	*500*
Name of Payee	*Alice Claywell*
Date Received	*September 28, 2003*

Payment Reason	Description	Check Amount	Cash Amount
Fund-Raising Event	*Vending—Soft Drinks*		*$100.00*
	(Staff machines)		
Field Trip			
Dues			
Textbook Fees			
Gym Suits			
Locks			
Other Fees			
	Subtotals	**$0.00**	**$100.00**
	Total		**$100.00**

Bonnie Heywood	*September 28, 2003*
Teacher/Sponsor's Signature	**Date Issued**

FORM 20-A

Vending Service Authorization and Financial Report

This form is used to record the principal's approval of vending service and to report financial information about the service at the end of the school year.

FORM 20-B

Individual Receipt (Vending Services)

This prenumbered, multicopy form is used to receipt money collected from a student, parent, or staff member for a variety of purposes. In this example, one vending sponsor (Alice Claywell) has counted the cash from the staff vending machine and she has turned it over to her cosponsor (Bonnie Heywood), who has counted the stock at the same time to determine the number of items sold. The sponsors attach documentation reconciling the items sold with the funds collected to a copy of the completed form, which they submit to the bookkeeper, along with the money. The other copies of the receipt remain in the vending receipt book, held by one of the sponsors.

Appendix C

A Guide to the CD-ROM

The CD-ROM accompanying this book provides downloadable versions of the sample forms presented in Appendix B. You are welcome to use them as templates for prenumbered forms or distribute and use them in your school. The forms have been created in Microsoft Excel, the leading spreadsheet software. Each form is presented in a separate document and has been designed for data entry and automatic calculation. Embedded prompts provide guidance on the type of information to enter in each field. Each document also contains a sample, filled-in version of the form, which reflects the print version of the examples presented in Appendix B.

Disk Contents

Name of the Electronic File		Text Example	Page
01	Ticket Sales Report	Form 2-A	127
02	Event Financial Report	Form 2-B	127
03	Bank Reconciliation Form	Form 3-A	128
04	Blanket Purchase Order (Purchasing/Credit Card Use)	Form 5-A	129
05	Encumbrance Tracking Spreadsheet	Form 7-A	129
06	Field Trip Authorization and Financial Report	Form 8-A	130
07	Individual Receipt (Field Trip)	Form 8-B	131
08	Group Receipt (Field Trip)	Form 8-C	132
09	Field Trip Permission Form	Form 8-D	132
10	Field Trip Checklist	Form 8-E	133
11	Fund-Raising Event Authorization and Financial Report	Form 9-A	134
12	Individual Receipt (Fund-Raising)	Form 9-B	135
13	Group Receipt (Fund-Raising)	Form 9-C	135
14	Fund-Raising Event Sponsor's Distribution List	Form 9-D	136
15	Petty Cash Reimbursement Voucher	Form 13-A	137
16	Petty Cash Reconciliation Form	Form 13-B	137
17	Raffle Ticket Sales Report	Form 14-A	138
18	Raffle Financial Report	Form 14-B	138

System Requirements

486 Pentium processor-based personal computer
Microsoft Windows 98, Windows NT 4.0, or later
Minimum RAM: 8 MB for Windows 98 and NT
Available space on hard disk: 8 MP Windows 98 and NT
2X speed CD-ROM drive or faster

Getting Started

Insert the CD-ROM into your computer's CD-ROM drive and click on the icon to launch. You will see a directory of the MS Excel documents.

To Download Documents

The documents on the CD-ROM are read-only. To download a document, open it by double-clicking on the document name. Under the File pull-down menu, choose Save As. Save the document onto your hard drive, using a new file name. It is important to use a different name; otherwise, the document may remain a read-only file.

To Use the Forms

Once you have saved the documents to your hard drive, follow the embedded instructions in each form to customize it for your school's use (e.g., adding your school's name). Please note that calculations in the forms are entry-protected. To change programming or calculation options, or to add or subtract cells and text, you will need to turn off the sheet protection. Consult MS Excel programming guidelines or the Help feature for specific instructions.

It is important that those responsible for reviewing and "signing off" on electronic financial forms that contain automated calculations remember to always give these forms the same degree of scrutiny they would give to old-fashioned paper forms. Finally, please note that forms for receipts and purchase orders should be used only as templates for creating prenumbered forms that are carefully controlled.

Glossary of School Accounting Terms

Activity funds—All internal school funds received and administered at the school level under the direction of the principal. For tracking purposes, activity funds fall into two categories: cash accounts and fund accounts. Activity funds can be used only for the purpose intended, but do not have to be spent in the year that they were raised. They usually have audit and reporting requirements specified by the district and state.

Activity fund safeguards—General accounting procedures designed to meet three important school financial objectives: (1) to protect school staff from suspicion of theft or laxness, (2) to protect school assets, and (3) to fulfill the stewardship responsibility for public funds expected by the general public.

Admission tickets—Prenumbered tickets sold to control entrance to a school event. Profits from the event are used to benefit a specific student group or the student body as a whole. Ticket sales apply to athletic events, school dances, school fairs, and other activities where admission to a school event is controlled.

Adjustment—A change to school bookkeeping records for the purpose of correcting a human error. Unauthorized adjustments to accounts could be a means of concealing theft.

Audit—A financial review of a school's activity funds and/or a performance review of its programs. A financial audit samples school records and determines how well the staff is following bookkeeping procedures and policies. An audit usually results in recommendations regarding bookkeeping procedures. Audit findings are normally reported to the district's central administration and to the school board.

Bank deposit register—A record of the amount to be deposited at the bank, based on the amount of money received that day.

Bank reconciliation—The process of ensuring that items listed on the school's bank statements (i.e., checking and savings accounts) accurately represent the information recorded in the school's books. The purpose of preparing the bank reconciliation is to identify differences between the bank's balance and the school's financial records (e.g., bank service charges, interest earned) and verify the reasons for the differences, based on written documentation.

Blanket purchase order—A written document that authorizes the purchase of a category of items (e.g., teacher supplies, office supplies, field day supplies), as long as the specified dollar amount of the purchase order is not exceeded. This type of purchase order is useful when it is necessary to buy small-dollar items and the exact items are not known at the time that the principal approves the purchase order. A staff member buys against the purchase order for a specified period of time until the authorized amount is spent.

Book fair—A fund-raising event that offers books and educational materials for sale to students and parents. Schools make a profit by agreeing with a vendor to a predetermined percentage of the total sales.

Bookkeeping—The tracking, through records, of incoming and outgoing funds in support of school activities under the direct control of the principal. The bookkeeping records are maintained daily by a bookkeeper, who is responsible for accurately and diligently adhering to procedures that apply to all staff members who handle school funds. The principal bears overall responsibility for ensuring compliance with the state and district accountability rules regarding these funds.

Categorical funds—Money allocated for a particular purpose. Use of these funds is restricted to certain educational activities, such as professional development, math instruction, or reading programs.

Cash accounts—A type of activity fund that designates the actual loca-

tion of school money: change funds, petty cash, checking accounts, and saving accounts. The total of all cash accounts must equal the total of all fund accounts.

Cash basis of accounting—The practice of recording money (cash and checks) at the time it is received by the school or paid out to a vendor. Purchases are only allowed when funds are sufficient to cover the purchase price.

Cash disbursements journal—A (normally computerized) report that gives the date a check was written, the check number, the name of the person or company being paid, the activity fund account that was reduced by the payment, and the dollar amount of the check. The cash disbursements journal is usually organized chronologically, based on the dates that checks were written.

Cash receipts journal—A summary report that indicates by date and receipt number the receipts that were issued by the office on a particular day.

Change fund—A limited fund of bills and coins intended to make small change when patrons are buying items such as admission tickets. Unlike a petty cash fund, the change fund is not used for reimbursement. The actual amount of a change fund must remain constant for the duration of the fund (e.g., $10 for an elementary school, $50 for a secondary school).

Credit/purchasing cards—A credit card obtained in the name of an administrator, school, or district for the purpose of charging school purchases or vendor-provided travel services. The intent of the card is to reduce the paper work associated with authorized school purchases. The principal's prior approval and the close monitoring of charged expenses are essential procedures to reduce the likelihood of fraudulent, improper, and questionable purchases.

Deposits in transit—Deposits recorded in the school's records that have been posted by the bank at a later date (e.g., end-of-the month receipts taken to the bank after 2:00 p.m. that are posted to the next business day or the first banking day of the next month). These deposits do not appear on the month's bank statement, but must be added in to reconcile the bank statement with the school's bookkeeping records.

Electronic banking transfer—A bank transaction that is initiated through an electronic terminal, telephone, computer, or magnetic tape for the purpose of authorizing a financial institution to add or deduct funds from an account. Electronic banking transfers allow schools to move money from one account to another without writing a traditional check to authorize the transaction.

Embezzlement—Unauthorized use of school funds in one's custody for personal gain. Accounting irregularities are used with the intent to conceal missing funds.

Encumbrances—The amount of money that has been obligated by a purchase order or similar document, such as a contract for services, before a check has been issued for payment. In an encumbrance system, a book-keeping entry records the estimated cost of a purchase at the time that a purchase order is issued. These funds are then considered expended and unavailable for other purchases or payments. The final expenditure is adjusted when the actual invoice is received. Encumbrances must be "tracked" to prevent overspending a school account.

FICA payroll taxes—Payroll deduction taxes that support the national system of Social Security payments. Full-time and part-time wages are subject to these taxes. The acronym "FICA" stands for the Federal Insurance Contributions Act of 1935, which established the Social Security program. Consult with your district payroll office regarding the timely payment of these taxes.

Financial report—A (usually computerized) report prepared monthly that shows the beginning balance, increases and decreases (including transfers/adjustments and encumbrances), and the ending balance for each account. The principal approves this report each month, along with the monthly bank statement. Differences between the monthly financial report and the monthly bank statement are reconciled with written bookkeeping documents.

Fidelity bonds—Insurance obtained by the school district that covers employees who handle school funds directly (e.g., a bookkeeper). The insurance reimburses the district for losses that result from an employee's dishonest actions on the job.

Field trips—Educational student trips sponsored by the school and directly related to the curriculum. Costs are paid for by parents, parent organizations, profits from fund-raising events, or the school's general fund. The purpose of collecting funds for a field trip is to cover expenses related to the trip, *not* to make money for the school.

Flow-through accounts—A type of activity fund for tracking money that the school collects on behalf of the central office (e.g., summer school tuition and fees for lost and damaged textbooks). Money in flow-through accounts is not for general school use and is sent to the district central office at the appropriate time.

Fraud—The willful misuse of school property or funds through misrepresentation or deception. The perpetrator usually benefits directly.

Fund accounts—A type of activity fund consisting of school accounts, student accounts, and flow-through accounts. Each fund category is designated for a particular purpose. The total of all fund accounts must equal the total of all cash accounts.

Fund-raising events of consumable supplies—Events sponsored by a school, individual club, or grade level to sell merchandise for the purpose of raising funds to benefit those students who participate in the fund-raising activity (e.g., the Honor Society's peanut sale to raise money for a field trip).

General ledger—A (usually computerized) bookkeeping report that provides detailed information on each school account. The report can be printed at any time, but it is usually printed at least once a month as part of general bookkeeping records. It can be printed for one account or all accounts, and for one month or all months to date. The general ledger is a good reference document for sponsors or administrators interested in obtaining detailed information on any account at any time.

Gifts to students or staff—Personal goods or services for students or staff purchased with school funds. Gifts include items purchased for the personal use of a student or staff member (e.g., baby shower items). Gifts exclude items purchased by the school or the district for the staff's use at school (e.g., bulletin board supplies, hand calculators, school desk accessories). Gifts should only come from funds collected specifically for this purpose (e.g., staff remembrance funds).

Grant funds—Funds given to the school by an organization, company, or government agency for use in a predetermined project or activity. Schools typically apply for these funds through a written application process. The use of grant funds is usually restricted. Most grants have time limits and reporting requirements.

Internal controls—General bookkeeping procedures designed to meet three important school financial objectives: (1) to protect school assets, (2) to protect school staff from suspicion of theft or laxness, and (3) to fulfill the stewardship responsibility expected by the general public.

Internal control questionnaire—A number of written questions about a school's current bookkeeping procedures (e.g., are school store receipts forwarded to the bookkeeper daily?) based on district policies and procedures. Auditors use this document as a basis for conducting a financial audit.

Interest earned—A percentage payment (e.g., 1–3 percent annually) that the school receives from the bank for maintaining a minimum balance in a bank account. Interest earned on an account appears on the bank statement. Interest earned must be added to the school's books in order to reconcile the bank balance with the school's balance.

Miscellaneous bank charges—Fees charged by banks for specially requested services that are not included in the monthly service charges (e.g., printing fees for deposit slips or checks). Miscellaneous bank charges appear on the monthly bank statement and must be subtracted from the school's books.

Miscellaneous deposits—Positive adjustments in the school's bank balance that the bank may grant for various reasons (e.g., refunding a previous service charge, corrections for deposit or check cashing errors made by the bank). These increases to the school account appear on the monthly bank statement.

Misuse—Inappropriate use of school funds where there is no benefit to the school or to the proper group of students.

Nonsufficient funds (NSF)—Charges incurred when a school deposits a check received from parents or staff members who do not have sufficient funds in their bank accounts to cover the amount of the check. In other words, a check received by the school "bounced." In these instances, the bank charges the deposit amount back to the school, along with a processing fee. These charges appear on the monthly bank statement.

Online purchasing—The process of ordering goods and services over the Internet. Safeguards must be in place to ensure the same degree of financial security that is available with paper purchase orders and "snail mail" processing.

Outstanding checks—Checks issued by the school that have not yet cleared the school's checking account (e.g., a check issued on the last day of the month may not clear the bank until the next month). These checks will have been subtracted from the school's balance, but will not appear on the current bank statement.

Packing slips—Documents included with shipments of ordered materials listing all items in the shipment and (usually) cost and shipping expenses. These papers should be matched against the purchase order to verify receipt of all items ordered. Packing slips are also called "receiving documents."

Parent organizations—Private, parent-run, nonprofit organizations that support school projects through the donation of money, equipment, and services. All parent organization funds are accounted for and reported separately from school activity funds. These organizations obtain nonprofit status in accordance with Internal Revenue Service (IRS) regulations.

Payment package—The collected documentation that justifies writing a check from school funds. This package may include the original vendor invoice or sales receipt, purchase order, packing slip, verification of services received, and any other documentation that substantiates the purchase.

Petty cash fund—A limited fund of bills and coins (e.g., $50–100) used to reimburse small, unexpected purchases in situations where it is impractical to issue frequent, individual checks. Procedures are necessary to protect the funds from misuse or theft.

Profit—The amount of funds from revenue-generating events (e.g., athletic competitions or fund-raising campaigns) available for use by the school or group of students after expenses have been paid.

Purchase order—A formal, pre-numbered multicopy document that authorizes the purchase of goods and services with school funds. A purchase order includes a description of the material ordered, the price, the specific account to be charged, and an administrator's signature. Schools "track" purchase orders to ensure that funds are available to pay the vendor when payment is due and that the items are received and paid for in a timely manner.

Purchase order status report—A computerized bookkeeping report that includes summary information, such as purchase order number, date of the order, the name of the person or company being issued the purchase order, the fund account that was charged with the encumbrance (i.e., the estimated amount of the purchase used to set aside funds), and the actual purchase order amount.

Raffle—A type of lottery in which individuals purchase one or more tickets in anticipation of winning an offered prize from a random drawing of tickets. Profits from the sale of prenumbered raffle tickets are used for the benefit of the entire school, a specific group of students or the staff. Federal and state regulations applicable to games of chance apply to school raffles.

Receiving documents—Documents included with shipments of ordered materials listing all items in the shipment and (usually) cost and shipping expenses. These papers should be matched against the purchase order to verify receipt of all items ordered. Receiving documents are also called "packing slips."

Reimbursement grants—A grant arrangement wherein the school spends its own money and then submits the bills to the granting agent. The granting agent pays back to the school the money spent, in accordance with the grant guidelines.

School budget—An estimate of the revenue and expenditures for a school year. All funds allocated to and raised by the school make up the school budget.

School store—A school-operated store where student supplies are sold. The inventory volume and items are based on school board procedures and the student population (e.g., gym suits for middle and high schools, pencils for elementary schools).

Service charge—The bank's fee for processing monthly account transac-

tions (e.g., the service charge may be based on the average daily balance in the bank account). This fee appears on the monthly bank statement.

Staff reimbursement—The process of "paying back" approved expenses that staff members incur on behalf of the school (e.g., purchase of school supplies, travel expenses). District guidelines usually determine both the maximum dollar amount that can be reimbursed at the school level and the procedures to follow.

Student activity accounts—Funds raised by student organizations (e.g., profits from the student government's bumper sticker sale) for use by a student group. These funds legally belong to the student group that raised the funds and may not be used for general school purposes.

Travel advance—Funds given to a staff member before a school-related trip to cover the estimated related costs. The staff member signs a form acknowledging that funds were received and that any amount not spent must be returned.

Transfer—A change to school bookkeeping accounts for the purpose of moving funds from one account to another. Unauthorized transfers between accounts could be a means of hiding theft of school funds.

Upfront grants—Grant arrangement wherein a school receives money in installments. A school is not required to spend its funds first and then submit bills for reimbursement.

Vending—A type of ongoing fund raising consisting of the sale of drinks or snacks from coin-operated machines. The profits from sales benefit either the students or staff, depending on where the machines are located and who purchases the items (e.g., teachers' lounge or student hallway).

References and Resources

ABC News. (2002, April 18). *The check's at the cleaners: How to protect your checks from being stolen or "washed."* Retrieved April 19, 2002, from http://abcnews.go.com/ sections/primetime/DailyNews/primetime_ checkwashing_feature.html.

Alliance for Nonprofit Management. (n.d.). *What internal controls are needed for cash disbursements?* Retrieved April 2001, from http://www.allianceonline.org/faqs/ fmfaq23.html.

Business Against Crime. (2001). Internal controls. In *Dealing with white collar crime* (part 6). Retrieved April 2001, from http://www. whitecollarcrime.co.za/dwc/5.htm.

Chesney, L. (1999, February). The heart of the matter. *Internal Auditor, 56,* 50–52.

Chicago Public Schools. (2002). Introduction. In *Internal accounts manual.* Retrieved September 6, 2002, from http://www.csc.k12. il.us/finance/Iamanual/ and available from Chicago Public Schools, Director of General Accounting, 125 S. Clark Street, 14th Floor, Chicago, IL 60603.

Code of Virginia. (2002). Sec 2.2-4377. Available through a searchable database at http:// leg1.state.va.us/000/src.htm.

Council of Chief State School Officers. (1996). *ISLLC standards for school leaders.* Retrieved July 15, 2002, from http://www.ccsso.org/ standrds.html.

Denver District Attorney's Office. (2001). *What you need to know about employee embezzlement.* Retrieved May 23, 2001, from http:// www.denverda.org/ecu__employee_ embezzlement.htm.

Federal Deposit Insurance Corporation. (1993). Part 205: Electronic fund transfers (Regulation E). *Consumer protection index.* Retrieved November 15, 2002, from http:// www.fdic.gov/regulations/laws/rules/6500-3100.html.

Federal Trade Commission. (2002, June). *Credit, ATM, and debit cards: What to do if they're lost or stolen.* Retrieved September 11, 2002, from http://www.ftc.gov/bcp/conline/ pubs/credit/atmcard.htm.

Fisher, P. M., Taylor, W. J., & Leer, A. J. (1982). *Advanced accounting* (2nd ed.). Cincinnati, OH: South-Western Publishing.

Fraud. (2002, August). *Journal of Accountancy, 194,* 18. Available: http://www.aicpa.org/ pubs/jofa/aug2002/news1.htm#7.

Georgetown University. (2002). Employee reimbursement form. In *Financial affairs manual.* Retrieved July 22, 2003, from http://www.georgetown.edu/ and available from Georgetown University, Office of Financial Affairs. 37th and O Street, NW, Washington, DC 20057.

Hardy, L. (1999, October). The lure of school marketing. *American School Board Journal, 22.* Retrieved May 2001, from http://www. asbj.com/199910/1099coverstory.html.

Institute of Internal Auditors. (2003). *Standards for the professional practice of internal auditing.* Altamonte Springs, FL: Author.

Available: http://www.theiia.org/ecm/ guidance.cfm?doc_id=1499.

Internal Revenue Service. (2000, December). *Topic 501(c)(3): Charitable contributions.* Retrieved July 22, 2003, from http://www.irs.gov.

Internal Revenue Service. (2002a). *General instructions for Form 1099.* Retrieved October 14, 2002, from http://www.irs.gov/pub/irs-pdf/i1099gi2.pdf.

Internal Revenue Service. (2002b). *Publication 505: Tax withholding and estimated tax.* Retrieved December 13, 2002, from http://www.irs.gov/pub/irs-pdf/p505.pdf.

Internal Revenue Service. (2002c). *Topic 419: Gambling income and expense.* Retrieved May 3, 2002, from http://www.irs.gov/taxtopics/page/0,,id=16211,00.html.

Internal Revenue Service. (2003a, January). Who are employees? In *Publication 15-A: Employer's supplemental tax guide* (chapter 1). Available: http://www.irs.gov/pub/irs-pdf/p15a.pdf.

Internal Revenue Service. (2003b, January). Wages and other compensation. In *Publication 15-A: Employer's supplemental tax guide* (chapter 5). Available: http://www.irs.gov/pub/irs-pdf/p15a.pdf.

Keys, T. E. (Ed.). (1999, June). Auditors never stop auditing. *Internal Auditor, 51,* 72–75.

Meigs, R. F., & Meigs, W. B. (1992). *Financial accounting* (7th ed.). New York: McGraw-Hill.

Mutter, D. W. (2002, July 18). *School money matters.* Paper presented at a meeting of the Virginia Association of Elementary School Principals Institute, Williamsburg, Virginia.

National PTA Annual Resources, 2000–2001. (2000, March). *Money matters: Financial management guide for PTAs.* Retrieved October 13, 2002, from http://www.pta.org.

O'Rourke, A. (May, 1998). Internal cash controls keep employees honest. *Appraisal Today.* Retrieved April 2001, from http://www.appraisaltoday.com/cash.htm.

Parker, P. (2001, May). *Effective internal controls for school activity funds.* Paper presented at the Virginia Association of School Business Officials Conference, Richmond, Virginia.

Parker, P. (2002, May). *Audits to go: School activity funds and transportation.* Paper presented at the National Association of Local Government Auditors National Conference, Tahoe, California. Notes retrieved September 24, 2002, from http://www.nalga.org/confer/tahoe02/presentations/Parker.doc.

Robertson, J. C. (2000). *Fraud examination for managers and auditors: 2nd edition.* Austin, TX: Viesca Books.

Sawyer, L., Dittenhofer, M., & Scheiner, J. (1996). *Sawyer's internal auditing* (4th ed.). Altamonte Springs, FL: Institute of Internal Auditors.

Sheehan, J. (1999, October). Why I said no to Coca-Cola. *American School Board Journal,* 25. Retrieved May, 2001, from http://www.asbj.com/199910/1099coverstory.html.

Sielke, C. C. (2002). A penny saved: Fund balance fundamentals. *American School Board Journal.* Retrieved December 12, 2002, from http://www.asbj.com/schoolspending/resourcessielke.html.

Stanford University. (2002, March 15). *Administrative guide: Purchasing cards.* Retrieved September 11, 2002, from http://www.search.stanford.edu.

Sweeney, P. (2002, July). Five tips to steer clear of the courthouse. *Internal Auditor, 194,* 34–38.

Thompson, C. (Ed.). (1999, August). Irreconcilable differences. *Internal Auditor, 51,* 71–73.

Thompson, D. C., & Wood, C. R. (1998). *Money and schools: A handbook for practitioners.* Larchmont, NY: Eye On Education.

U.S. General Accounting Office. (1999). *Government auditing standards.* Washington, DC: U.S. Government Printing Office. Available: http://www.gao.gov/govaud/ybk01.htm.

U.S. General Accounting Office. (2002). *Government purchase cards: Control weaknesses expose agencies to fraud and abuse* (GAO, 02-676T). Washington, DC: U.S. Government Printing Office. Available http://www.gao.gov/new.items/d02676t.pdf.

University of Florida. (2000). Purchasing cards. In *Handbook on business procedure.* Retrieved September 6, 2002, from http://www.ufl.edu and available from the Office of the Vice President of Finance and Administration, University of Florida, Gainesville, FL 32611.

University of Virginia. (2002, November). Petty cash, petty cash checking, and change funds. In *Financial and administrative policies and procedures* (policy 2-e). Retrieved December 10, 2002, from http://www.virginia.edu/finance/polproc/pol/iie2.html.

Vail, K. (1998, May). Eleven ways to make money: When traditional funding isn't enough, many school districts become entrepreneurs. *American School Board Journal, 6,* 30–31.

Vail, K. (1999, February). Insert coins in slot: School vending machines generate funds—and controversy. *American School Board Journal, 28.* Retrieved May 14, 2001, from http://www.asbj.com/199902/0299expresslines.html.

Virginia Commonwealth University. (2002). Departmental Petty Cash. In *Financial and budget administration policies and procedures manual* (chapter 5). Retrieved December 10, 2002, from http://www.vcu.edu/treasury/pettycash.htm.

Virginia Department of Education. (1989). *School activity funds.* Richmond, VA: Author. Available from Financial Services, Commonwealth of Virginia Department of Education, P.O. Box 2120, Richmond, VA 23218-2120.

Walsh-Sarnecki, P., Schaeffer, J., & Ross, J. (2000, November 21). Detroit school audits brings embezzlement charges. *Detroit Free Press.* Retrieved January 22, 2001, from http://www.freep.com.

Washoe County (Nev.) Government. (1996). *Washoe County internal control procedures manual.* Available from Internal Audit Department, Washoe County, P.O. Box 11130, 1001 E. 9th Street, Reno, NV 89520.

Watts, J. C., Burkel, D. V., & Watts, O. (2001). The buck really does stop in the principal's office. *National Forum of Educational Administration and Supervision Journal.* Retrieved April 10, 2001, from http://www.nationalforum.com/21/watts.htm.

Wells, J. T. (2001, July). And nothing but the truth: Uncovering fraudulent disclosures (The Fraud Beat). *Journal of Accountancy, 192,* 47–52.

Wells, J. T. (2002a, August). Billing schemes, part 2: Pass-throughs. *Journal of Accountancy, 194,* 72–74.

Wells, J. T. (2002b, September). Billing schemes, part 3: Pay-and-return invoicing. *Journal of Accountancy, 194,* 96–98.

Zorn, R. L. (1999, February). The great cola wars: How one district profits from competition for vending machines. *American School Board Journal, 31.* Retrieved May 14, 2001, from http://www.asbj.com/199902/0299expresslines.html.

Index

Note: An *f* following a page number indicates a figure. Bolded numbers indicate a chapter-length discussion of the topic.

About the Authors

Davida W. Mutter is a partner and consultant with School Solutions, an organization in Chesapeake, Virginia, that provides school districts with school finance, program evaluation, and school improvement services. She began her career in public education as a teacher, and during 19 of the next 30 years, served in the Chesapeake (Va.) Public Schools (a system of 39,000 students) in a variety of positions, including Assistant Superintendent for Budget and Finance, Director of Budget, Director of Accounting, Director of Internal Audit, Director of Program Evaluation, and Director of Staff Development. She retired as a full-time administrator in 2000.

Davida holds a doctorate from the University of Massachusetts at Amherst, a master of arts from the College of William and Mary, and a bachelor of science in elementary education from Old Dominion University. She has presented at the National School Board Conference and the National Elementary Principals Association Conference, as well as at workshops for administrators and teachers sponsored by the Virginia Association of Elementary School Principals.

During the past 15 years, Davida has published articles on a wide range of administrative topics in the *American School Board Journal, Journal of School Facility Planners, School Business Affairs,* and *ERS Spectrum.* She is currently co-authoring a new book on program evaluation.

Davida may be reached at dmutter@cox.net or School Solutions, 621 Caleb Drive, Chesapeake, Virginia 23322.

Pam J. Parker is a former Chief Internal Auditor for Chesapeake Public Schools in Chesapeake, Virginia, having retired in 2002. She is a certified public accountant and a certified internal auditor. Pam holds a master's degree in business administration from the University of Southern Mississippi and a bachelor of science degree from Limestone College.

Pam began her extensive career in accounting and auditing in private industry, serving in professional positions with Hoshizaki America, NASA, Alcoa, and Healthtex Apparel Corp. before moving to public education as Assistant Director of Accounting and Chief Internal Auditor in Chesapeake Public Schools.

As a professional auditor, Pam started the Local School Auditors Association in Hampton Roads. She is a past president of the Virginia Local Government Auditors Association and a member of the American Institute of Certified Public Accountants, the South Carolina Association of Certified Public Accountants, the Institute of Internal Auditors, and the Virginia Association of School Business Officials. She is a past director of the Institute of Management Accountants.

Pam has spoken at conferences held by the Virginia Association of School Business Officials, the Virginia Association of Elementary School Principals, the Virginia Department of Education, and the National Association of Governmental Auditors.

Pam may be reached at PJParkerCPA@aol.com or 4490 Chatham Road, Suffolk, Virginia 23435.

Related ASCD Resources for Principals and Aspiring Principals

Audiotapes

Becoming a Standards Based Principal by Judy Aaronson and Marge Sable (#200108)
Elements of Successful Staff Development: The Principal's Role by Irv Richardson (#299142)
Successful Strategies for New Principals by Karen Dyer (#297186)
Mentoring the Assistant Principal by Pam Robbins (#203078)

Multimedia

Analytic Processes for School Leaders: An ASCD Action Tool by Cynthia T. Richetti and Benjamin B. Tregoe (#701016)
Promoting Learning Through Student Data: An ASCD Profession Inquiry Kit by Marian Leibowitz (#999004)

Online Professional Development

Go to ASCD's Home page (http://www.ascd.org) and click on Professional Development. ASCD Professional Development Online Courses include "Effective Leadership," "Parents as Partners in Schooling," and "How to Evaluate Professional Development."

Print Products

Communicating with the Public: A Guide for School Leaders by Anne Meek (#199052)
Energize Your Meetings with Laughter by Sheila Feigelson (#198055)
How to Prepare for and Respond to a Crisis by David J. Schonfeld, Robert Lichtenstein, Marsha Kline Pruett, and Dee Speese-Linehan (#103029)
Keeping Good Teachers by Marge Scherer (#104138)
Leadership for Learning: How to Help Teachers Succeed by Carl D. Glickman (#101031)
Lessons from Exceptional School Leaders by Mark F. Goldberg (#101229)
Motivating Students and Teachers in an Era of Standards by Richard Sagor (#103009)
Principals and Student Achievement: What the Research Says by Kathleen Cotton (#103309)

Videotapes

The Principal Series (7-tape series with 2 facilitator's guides) (#499242)
The Principal Series, Tapes 1–3 (with facilitator's guide)(#498200)
The Principal Series, Tape 5: The Principal as Manager (with facilitator's guide) (#499239)

For additional resources, visit us on the World Wide Web (http://www.ascd.org), send an e-mail message to member@ascd.org, call the ASCD Service Center (1-800-933-ASCD or 703-578-9600, then press 2), send a fax to 703-575-5400, or write to Information Services, ASCD, 1703 N. Beauregard St., Alexandria, VA 22311-1714 USA.